JARGON 64

ST. EOM
IN THE LAND
OF
PASAQUAN

The Life and Times and Art of
EDDIE OWENS MARTIN

as told to & recorded by
TOM PATTERSON

photography by Jonathan Williams,
Roger Manley, Guy Mendes
foreword by John Russell

THE JARGON SOCIETY

Library of Congress Catalog Card Number: 87-80710
ISBN (Cloth): 0-912330-60-0
ISBN (Subscribers' Edition): 0-912330-61-9

Designed by Tom Patterson and
Jonathan Williams

Typesetting by Monotype Composition, Baltimore, Maryland
Printed and bound
in Japan

Distributed by
Inland Book Company,
22 Hemingway Avenue
East Haven, Connecticut 06512
Toll-free (800) 243-0138

The Jargon Society wishes to thank the following for their sponsorship of, or other assistance with, the preparation and publication of this title: Donald B. Anderson, John P. Hunter, Jr., The Lubo Fund, the City of Atlanta Bureau of Cultural Affairs, the North Carolina Arts Council, the Southern Arts Federation, the John Wesley & Anna Hodgin Hanes Foundation, the Z. Smith Reynolds Foundation, the Lyndhurst Foundation, the Columbus Museum, *Art Papers*, Mrs. Dewey Patterson, Mr. & Mrs. T. K. Patterson, Fred Fussell, Scotty Steward, Mrs. Ruth Martin, Dana Atchley, Lucinda Bunnen, Virginia Warren Smith, Roger Manley, Ted Potter, SPACES, President Jimmy Carter, Suzanne Jones.

Portions of the text from *St. EOM in The Land of Pasaquan* have previously appeared in different form in *Art Papers* and *BOMB* magazine.

A portion of the proceeds from sales of this book will be set aside to help support the preservation and maintenance of the Pasaquan site in Marion County, Georgia, through the Pasaquan Preservation Fund of the Columbus Museum. Inquiries and tax-deductible contributions should be directed to: Fred Fussell, Chief Curator, The Columbus Museum, P.O. Box 1617, Columbus, Georgia 31902.

to the memory of St. EOM (1908-1986)

CONTENTS

FOREWORD

This is on every count a most peculiar book. In the patois of today, it is "very unique." Not only does it violate every canon of taste and propriety, but it puts all the traditional family values through the wringer (Only to the mother/son relationship is a certain respect accorded). Few will argue with Tom Patterson's general estimate of Eddie Owens Martin's conversational style—that, "refusing to be patronized or intimidated, he talked like a campy, trash-mouthed, 1930s Harlem hipster."

He had a great deal to say, moreover, and it was of a kind not often encountered in polite society. ("Ever since I can remember," he tells us, "I was interested in sex. It never seemed strange to me. I was *born* ready to go.") We should also note a key passage that occurs not far into the book. When he was twelve, or maybe thirteen, Eddie Martin went out of the family house in Marion County, Georgia on a night when there was a full moon. With a tasseled piano scarf wrapped around his head, he knelt down in a plum bush thicket and prayed to God to make him different from anyone else in the world. "And by God," he said to Tom Patterson, "I think I succeeded in that prayer."

Not only was his prayer answered, but he set down the consequences of it without shame or abatement. He was completely, integrally, irreducibly himself. He lived his own particular kind of American dream, and he was beholden to nobody while doing it. For anything comparable to his story, and to the attitudes that he personified, we should have to go to the epigrams of Martial in the 1st century A.D., or to "Monsieur Nicolas" (1794–95) by Restif de la Bretonne, or to the first-hand accounts of the wandering, near-criminal life as it was lived in 18th and early 19th century France that have lately been dredged out of the archives by a British historian, Richard Cobb. When it comes to baring his heart (and other parts of his person) Eddie Martin went as far as any of them.

Quite apart from that, he was a master of context. When we are through reading this book, we know what it was like to grow up in the South in the early years of this century as one of seven children born into a poor-white-trash sharecropper's family. "A Caucasian cracker with some Indian blood on his mother's side," to quote Tom Patterson's summation, he was at home with black people, all his life long, and much preferred them to whites. In this way he moved, almost as an invisible man (or, at any rate, as an unidentifiable one), from one faction to another in the vast, city-wide conspiracy to outwit the law that was the mark of New York in the 1920s. He worked the streets. He worked the theater district. He worked the nightworld of Harlem. He was hustler, pusher, bartender, professional gambler. He rode the freight trains during the Depression. Sentenced to a year in the old Federal Narcotics Prison in Lexington, Kentucky, he turned his term there into an upside-down Arcadia in which drugs were free, sex could be had for the asking in the tops of shady trees and a little light gardening was all that the authorities demanded.

Released in 1943, he graduated into fortune-telling, for which he showed a remarkable aptitude. It was not that he mastered the standard techniques of tea-leaf and playing card, but that he functioned from instinct as what he called "a poor man's psychiatrist." For just a little money, he took people who came in "puzzled and all in a whirl" and broke down their troubles into a few words of common sense. Himself rarely or never touched by what is generally understood to be love, he believed that " 'love' is a word that should be abolished from the language, and it oughtta be replaced with 'respect' instead."

In this and many another passage in the later part of the book we recognize that Eddie Martin, who for the first half of his life was anesthetized to what is usually considered as morality, turned with time into someone who functioned in relation to other people as a deeply moral and constructive human being. This he owed to a revelation that came to him in 1935 at a time of grave physical illness. "Now that I'm older," he said to Tom Patterson, "I realize that my spirit had done left my body and took a spiritual journey. . . . I felt regenerated. Renewed. And it was then that I decided to be myself, regardless of the cost, regardless of the ostracism. Because, believe me, you get plenty of flak, man."

As to what came of that decision, this book has much to say. Hereinafter called St. EOM, he was nonetheless always the same all-seeing, all-intuiting and completely insubordinate Eddie Owens Martin. He treated everyone with the wary, watchful attentiveness that had served him well in many a tight corner. But he lived, in fact though not in name, the life of a healer. After he moved in the 1950s to a phantasmagorical compound that he had built near Buena Vista, Georgia, it was nothing for him to have eight, nine or ten carloads of eager clients waiting for him to get out of bed and tell their fortunes. Once they got in, he never failed them.

As will be clear from this book, that compound was, and doubtless is, an astonishing sight. Once St. EOM had got religion, he got every religion that there ever had been. He read about them, looked up their architecture in libraries (not least, that of the Metropolitan Museum, whose strangest-looking habitué he must have been), and pored over the paintings and sculptures to which they had given rise. All time and all places fed his imagination. First as a painter, and later as a combination of builder, sculptor and decorator, he turned his property into a combination of fortress, temple and dance platform. He also built up for himself what Tom Patterson calls "an extensive wardrobe of ceremonial drag," thereby persisting in a domain of effort where he had always excelled. (The drag balls of the 1920s had had no more inventive adherent than he.)

In time, what Tom Patterson calls his "psychedelic Assisi in the Southern pines" began to get talked about. Folk-art enthusiasts who turned up to gape, uninvited, were likely to get the bum's rush, thanks in part to two formidable German shepherds. Arts bureaucrats fared little better, though St. EOM did once allow himself to be inveigled into going to Washington, D.C., as part of an official deputation (with results that lose nothing in the telling). A visit from Former President Carter, in company with Mrs. Carter and their daughter Amy, went off better than might have been expected, given the tenor of the talk. (St. EOM "said a few words to him about why he got beat outta the White House that last time. I told him that Reagan's got just what this country wants: a good head o' hair and a mean line o' talk. And I asked him why he didn't do more things when he was in the seat of power.")

The Carters had come, like many others, to see not only what kind of marvel St. EOM had wrought, but what manner of man he could be. For his part, St. EOM didn't care who came, and would have been just as happy, if not happier, talking to the tall painted figures outside the back door of his house—or, for that matter, to the bales of straw that he was heard to interrogate during the last days of his life. "I built this place," he said, "to have something to identify with. Here I can be in my own world, with my temples and designs and the spirit of God. I can have my own spirits and my own thoughts. I don't have nothin' against other people and their beliefs. I'm not askin' anybody to do my way or be my way." And that's how it was, to the end.

It must be said for St. EOM that even in his most unregenerate days he was never messy in his private relations. Outrageous he may have been, but he was also prompt and decisive in the manner of his going. And so it was when, in April 1986, he no longer wished to live. Decisive to the last, he took his revolver and fired one shot into his temple. A Roman death, one might say. But what an American life!

John Russell
New York City
May 11, 1987

Buena Vista and Marion County, Georgia, early 1980's
Photographs by Guy Mendes

A NEIGHBOR'S EPIGRAPH:

IT'S NOT NOTHIN' LOCAL

"The first time I saw Eddie Martin was, oh, 30 or 40 years ago. Me and my husband had a little store up in the country not far from his mama's house, and he come in to buy a pair of work gloves one day. At first I was scared of him. I hadn't ever seen anybody that looked like that, with all that hair and that long beard. And skin just as smooth as a baby's. After a while I got used to seein' him around, though, and I wasn't scared of him any more. He keeps to himself pretty much. He's built all them things out there around his house, but he must not want nobody to see 'em, 'cause he's got all that cane planted so tall and thick you can't see the place even when you drive right by it. I think all that stuff he's built was influenced by the Indians. Whatever it is, it's not nothin' local. But it sure is pretty."

Mrs. Claudia Jones, a clerk at Parker's
Dry Goods, overlooking the courthouse
square in Buena Vista, Georgia,
June, 1984

INTRODUCTION

THE BLACKTOP ROAD TO PASAQUAN

A lot of us who have lived for more than a few years in the American South like to gripe about how the region looks too much like every other part of the country these days. The entire territory, we complain, seems to have been overrun by six-lane strips of asphalt lined with endless rows of the same gas stations and shopping malls and generic fast-food emporiums and flashing portable marquee signs that one sees anywhere else in the so-called "Sunbelt." But off the interstate highways and traffic-jammed franchise arteries, it is still in fact possible to find little pockets of what might be called The Real South—the kinds of places and people that gave this region its reputation as somehow very different from the rest of the U.S.A.

The Real South is a land of extremes, of paradox and contrast. At the same time that this part of the country has traditionally been an arch-conservative hotbed of uptight, Bible-thumping WASP fundamentalists, it has also always been a breeding ground for eccentrics and innovators of all kinds—the characters the straightlaced neighbors might regard with a little awe and suspicion. This is, after all, the territory which produced Little Richard, Elvis Presley, William Faulkner, Jasper Johns, George

Jones, James Brown, Tennessee Williams, Professor Longhair and the B-52s.

The realm which is explored in the following pages, created by one Eddie Owens Martin (a.k.a. "Saint EOM"), is called "Pasaquan," and it exists right now, off the main post-modern American highways on the far and isolated edge of the Wild and Eccentric Side of the Southern Paradox, in Marion County, Georgia.

Marion County and the whole stretch of country between the Ocmulgee and Chattahoochee rivers is a lonely, desolate landscape. The few small towns along the network of state and county roads in this area look all but abandoned, and the land itself has been ravaged by the timber companies so thoroughly that as far as the eye can see there's not much in the way of vegetation but dwarf oaks and spindly slash pines waiting in military rows to be harvested by Big Agribusiness.

Those great lady writers of the Dixie Bizarre School, Flannery O'Connor and Carson McCullers, came from nearby Georgia towns (Milledgeville and Columbus, respectively). And while both women had a real flair for portraying their neighbors' more outrageous quirks and obsessions, neither of them managed ever to concoct a character as outlandish as Eddie Owens Martin or a setting as odd as the compound of temples and pagodas and shrines to the gods of lost civilizations that he built around his century-old farmhouse in the pine barrens. Perhaps if Ms. O'Connor and Ms. McCullers had ingested fistfuls of the hallucinogenic psilocybe mushrooms that grow in the South Georgia cow pastures, then set about a collaborative rewrite of L. Frank Baum's *The Wizard of Oz,* they might have come close. But it's not likely.

Hang on tight, then, while you're snatched up as if by a cyclone and spirited away through the New Deep South and into another world at the end of the blacktop road—a rainbow-hued visionary monument that seems to belong to some forgotten culture in a far-off place and time. Welcome to the Land of Pasaquan, until recently the exclusive domain of its creator, the wizard/shaman/artist/builder E. O. Martin: St. EOM, self-annointed High Priest of his very own one-man religion, which he called "Pasaquoyanism."

One day more than 50 years ago Eddie Martin heard a voice, from "the spirit world," and that voice told him, "You're gonna be the start of somethin' new, and you're gonna be called a *Pasaquoyan,* and your name will be *Saint EOM.*" (The 'E' is silent, so it's pronounced like the ancient Eastern chant, *Om,* or the unit of electrical resistance, *ohm.*) "I heard that voice a long time before I knew any Spanish," St. EOM explained, "but later I found out that *pasa* means 'pass' in Spanish. And I found out that *quoyan* is an Oriental word that means 'bringin' the past and the future together, so you can derive the benefits of the past by bringin' it into the future.' And so I call myself a Pasaquoyan, and this place is called Pasaquan, where the past and the present and the future and everything else come together."

Situated on a remote, pine-shrouded ridge a few miles outside the little town of Buena Vista (pronounced "Bewna Vista" by its 1,500 citizens), Pasaquan is not an easy place to find. There's no mistaking it for anyplace else, though. It is a wild and dazzling patch of living, local hypertechnicolor, and seeing it for the first time is a mind-stretching experience indeed.

Eddie Martin was born and raised here in Marion County, less than 10 miles away, but even as a child he always felt somehow estranged, different from the other God-fearing citizens in this part of the Bible Belt. He was the archetypal kid who had his sights set on broader horizons. During his youth the neighbors didn't take any particular notice of him, since he was to all appearances just another barefoot plowboy in overalls. But by the time of his death at age 77 he was well accustomed to being regarded as the county's oddest character—"that crazy old fortune-teller Eddie Martin, who lives behind them weird-looking walls out toward Cusseta."

In the world outside Marion County, St. EOM received a bit of attention during the last decade of his life as a curiosity among environmental folk artists, but few of the people who take an interest in such things actually met him or saw his work firsthand. The folk enthusiasts are generally used to tamer, quainter folk artists than Eddie Martin, who came on strong. He had no use for "curriculum people," as he called the art and folklore academics. Refusing to be patronized or intimidated, he talked like a campy, trash-mouthed, 1930s Harlem hipster, and he was known to scare off visitors whose attitudes he didn't like. As for the citizens of Marion County, they treated Eddie Martin with a certain degree of ambivalent respect, but they didn't often use the word "artist" to describe him.

Imagine if you can a cross between Walt Whitman, Sun Ra, the Aztec emperor Moctezuma, Lord Buckley and Boy George, and you begin to get an idea of what sort of individual St. EOM was. An imposing figure, barrel-chested and six feet tall, he hadn't cut his hair or trimmed his beard in years, and what there was left of them was gray and worked into braids that were pulled up and bound together at the top of his skull. His extensive wardrobe of ceremonial drag was made up of long flowing robes and capes in brilliant multiple colors, candy-striped turbans and feathered headdresses, boots and bracelets trimmed with bells and seashells, naugahyde vests adorned with target shapes and tufts of black horsehair, and other similarly flashy outfits. He usually wore long sleeves to cover the blue tattoos running up and down each arm.

Pasaquan, St. EOM's psychedelic Assisi in the Southern pines, is a subtly balanced, garishly harmonious architectural compound which seems to have been built for the elaborate rituals of some long-vanished cult. Its temples, pagodas, shrines, altars, walls and walkways are embellished with cement-sculpted totem faces larger than life, swirling mandalas and occult-looking symbology, giant undulating snakes and Polynesian-like male and female figures in a variety of poses. All of this is painted in the brightest shades of Sherwin-Williams St. EOM could find in the local hardware store. Set on four acres and surrounded by miles of sparsely-populated, low-lying hill country, Pasaquan is carefully landscaped and strategically planted with thickets of tall bamboo and ribbon cane, which enhance the Oriental ambience while concealing the place from view of the pulpwood trucks, pickups and occasional cars that pass by on the blacktop country road. St. EOM said that in building it he was influenced by the ruined temple complexes of Pre-Columbian Mexico and his notion of what the civilizations on the fabled lost continents of Mu and Atlantis might have looked like. In some of its aspects Pasaquan calls to mind African sculpture and the statuary on Easter Island. And with its bold designs and flamboyant colors it also has the immediate impact of a carnival sideshow. Whatever the architect's intentions, the overall effect is that of a scaled-down Angkor Wat or Oz or Chichen Itza in some crazed 3-D cartoon, and it has left many a first-time visitor open-mouthed and speechless for long stretches of a morning or an afternoon.

So what's the story on this St. EOM character? Who was he, and why did he go to the trouble of building such things? We'll leave the detailed answers to those questions up to the Pasaquoyan himself, in the narrative that follows. By way of introduction to which I offer a few basic facts and observations:

Eddie Owens Martin was one of seven children born into a poor-white-trash sharecropper's family shortly after the turn of the century, and he wasn't the sort of boy who was about to be kept down on the farm. A runaway at the tender age of 14, he hit the streets of New York at the beginning of the Roaring Twenties. Like many a starry-eyed country boy who has run away to the big city, he turned to his only immediately available asset for making a living in a place where farm skills meant nothing—his body. He spent his first dozen years in New York as a midnight-cowboy-style street hustler. Later he made ends meet by running an illicit gambling parlor, dealing marijuana, working as a waiter in a gay nightclub, and finally by establishing himself as a fortune-teller on 42nd Street. By the time he was 30 years old he had decided that his real calling in life was art, and he spent much of his time during his last 20 years in

New York producing paintings and drawings which he was consistently unsuccessful in selling.

In many ways he was a man ahead of his time. Long before the eras of the beats, the rock-&-rollers, the hippies and the new-wavers, Eddie Martin had "done it all"—hitchhiking and freight-hopping across America, wearing strange clothes and hairstyles, dodging the draft, freewheeling sexual experimentation, dabbling in Eastern religions and the occult—you name it. When he finally returned to Georgia for good in the late 1950's, it wasn't to blend in discreetly with the rest of the local population, but rather to establish himself as a proudly hermetic recluse in self-imposed exile from the larger American society. He maintained that posture for 30 years, continuing to tell fortunes for a living while he built the *Paradiso* of his dreams. He was a man who felt he had Something to Prove, and his way of proving it was to create one of the most distinctive environmental artworks in America, a site which is comparable in range and scope and weirdness only to a few others in this country—Simon Rodia's Watts Towers in Los Angeles, Dinsmoor's Garden of Eden in Kansas and Howard Finster's Paradise Garden, also in Georgia. Never one to feign humility, St. EOM bitched until his dying day that he didn't receive the recognition he was due as an artist.

During St. EOM's last few years at Pasaquan his health began to decline along with his spirits. Then in April of 1986 he brought his extraordinary career to its startling conclusion with a single bullet from a .38-caliber pistol.

I first met St. EOM in 1980, when I made my first visit to Pasaquan with Jonathan Williams. The experience was, to put it mildly, astonishing, and after this first encounter with the man and his work I felt compelled to return to Pasaquan periodically, if only to reassure myself that I hadn't dreamed it all. Atlanta, where I lived at the time, was only a couple of hours away by car. After I had paid him five or six visits, Eddie slowly began to accept me as a friend, and he seemed pleased with the magazine piece I wrote about him in 1981, probably because it consisted mostly of direct quotes. He loved to hold forth, whether telling stories about his unconventional life or railing against the greed and stupidity of modern society, and I was always a willing audience, ready to listen to whatever he had to say or to sing. It wasn't uncommon for him to break suddenly into a guttural blues-chant in mid-conversation, putting into spontaneous rhyme anything that happened to be on his mind.

I had known Eddie for about three years when he phoned me up one morning to announce that he had decided to start working on his autobiography. He wanted to know if I would help him get it written and in print. I agreed without hesitation. My only regret, in retrospect, is that I wasn't able to finish my part of this collaboration in time for him to have seen the published results.

The Great High Pasaquoyan is gone, and the backwoods explorer in search of Wild Art and Architecture is now confronted only with this strange place he built in the middle of the American Nowhere.

To set the scene for the photographic tour that follows, I can only describe what an introductory visit to Pasaquan was like during the last years of its creator's life:

St. EOM didn't often take kindly to sightseers, and for many years he had as his constant companions two big German shepherds, just in case he needed any help in sending unwanted visitors on their way. In the driveway just outside the totem-flanked gateway was a hand-lettered sign that read, "BEWARE OF BAD DOGS. BLOW HORN AND WAIT IN CAR UNTIL *I COME OUT*." After driving up and following these instructions, you were liable to have to wait a half-hour or more before St. EOM let out a blood-curdling "shaman yell" from inside the gates, then paraded out in full tribal regalia with his dogs. While he sized you up to see what kind of "viberations" you gave off, the dogs snarled and bared their fangs. Their jaws looked strong enough to decapitate a medium-sized child with one chomp. When you asked if it was safe to get out of your car, St. EOM would say, "Them dogs won't mess with you, man. Not if you don't have no evil thoughts."

After pondering that response for as long as necessary, you decided whether you wanted to enter the Land of Pasaquan and the world of Eddie Owens Martin.

Photographs by Roger Manley

Photographs by Jonathan Williams

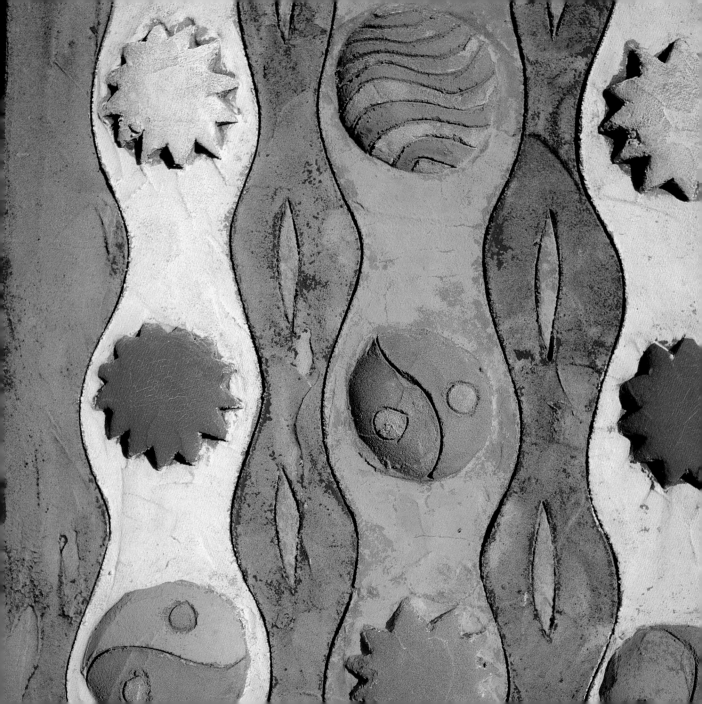

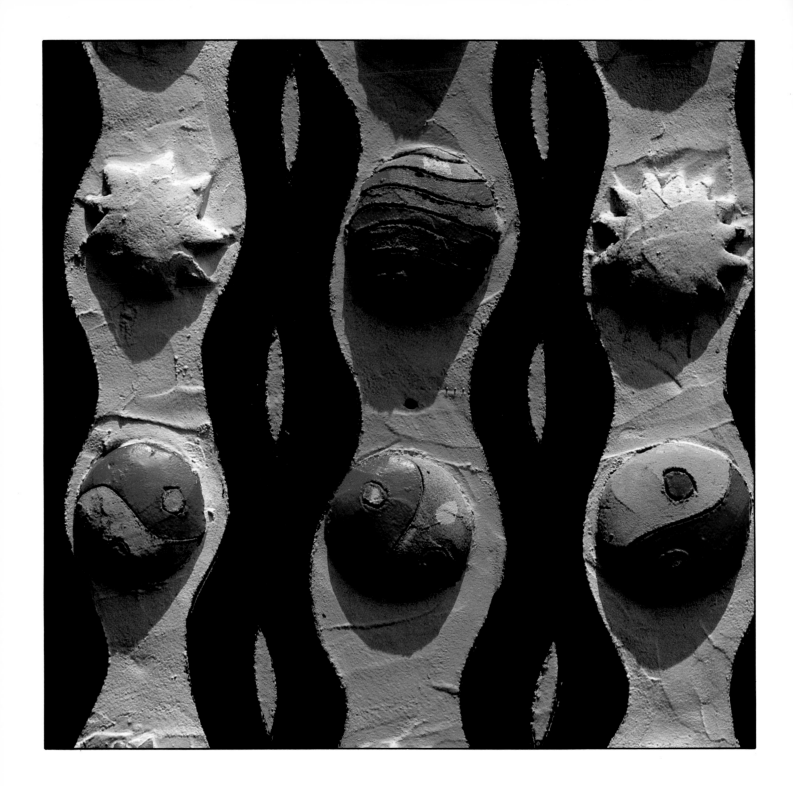

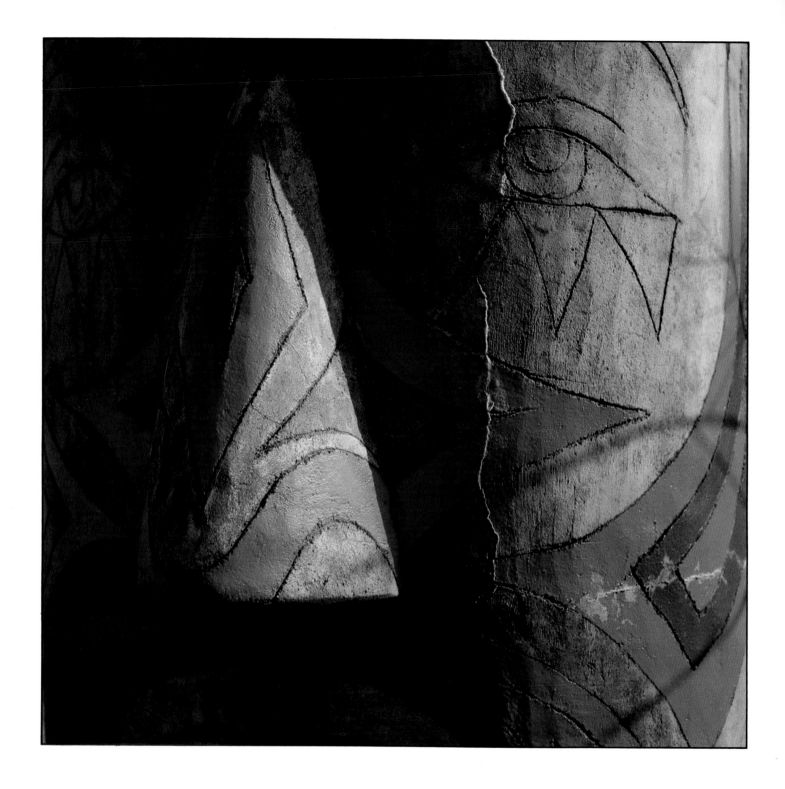

Take The EOM Train (Author's Note)

The text that follows is based on a long series of conversations with St. EOM beginning on his 75th birthday—July Fourth, 1983. On and off over the last three years of his life we sat for hours on end at the round table in the kitchen at Pasaquan, surrounded even in this seemingly domestic spot by blazing rainbow-colored murals and sculpture. There was often a big vat of collard greens or chicken and dumplings simmering on the stove, and a few mockingbirds were typically jabbering in the big oak just outside the window, taunting the assorted unnamed cats and kittens that lived around and under the house. All these sounds—boiling food, babbling birds, mewing felines—were picked up along with our voices by the tape machine. Listening to these tapes now, I can almost smell the greens cooking. St. EOM's voice is expressive and melodious, and his talk is sprinkled with spontaneous poetry, bawdy asides and hipster jive. Although by birth he was a Caucasian cracker with some Indian blood on his mother's side, St. EOM's voice sounded more black than white. The music of his speech was bluesy jazz, not country twang.

Virtually every word in the text is straight from the Pasaquoyan's mouth. It's only the sequencing of his anecdotes that I've fiddled with, for the sake of chronological continuity. So this is in effect an as-told-to auto-biography, in the form of a wide-ranging, amazingly candid and outrageous monologue, a running first-person account of the life of one stubbornly individualistic backwoods genius. There was certainly no need for me to "add color" to St. EOM's account of himself. Neither did I see any need to tone down or clean up his act. So the reader gets it straight: 100-proof, undiluted EOM.

As I write, putting the finishing touches on this manuscript on a rainy spring night in North Carolina, I'm sipping the house red and listening to Duke Ellington, Early Pasaquoyan Mood Music to set the appropriate tone. It has been almost three years since I embarked on this project, and more than six years since I first met the late High Priest of Pasaquoyanism. EOM may have been no saint in the Catholic sense, and lots of "decent American folk" will no doubt be appalled by much of his story. But he was an undisputably powerful artist, an instinctively sensitive architect, and a Genu-ine First Class Character in the great tradition of Southern eccentrics and raconteurs.

Picture it, then. It's a clear, hot, lazy afternoon in the Georgia pine barrens, early 1980s, and you're in the kitchen at Pasaquan, amidst all those resplendent floor-to-ceiling frescoes depicting mystical-looking characters in tropical settings. Across the table sits this terrifyingly wise-and-weary-looking Rabelaisian figure in a red t-shirt and a 10-gallon straw hat adorned with a hawk's wing, puffing on a fat spliff of some secret Pasaquoyan herbal mixture as he begins his autobiographical tale.

1. HOW DID I GET HERE?

I was born at home, on the Fourth of July, 1908, right here in Marion County. My mother's mother brought me into this world. She was a midwife. And until I was 14 years old I lived just a few miles from here, in a little village called Glen Alta.

Glen Alta was just a little train stop out in the country, with nothin' but woods and farmland for miles all around. There was a country store and a few houses down by the railroad track, and a freight house and a waitin' room for passengers who were gon' ride the train to Columbus or wherever they were goin'. And that was the life there. Everybody farmed, and some of 'em worked at the sawmill, and some of 'em worked at the gin when they were ginnin' cotton. But most of 'em were sharecroppers like we was. We lived up the hill and across the tracks from the store and the waitin' room, hollerin' distance from a few neighbors. You didn't hardly know nobody that lived over three or four hills from you. The only time

99

you'd come in contact with 'em was when you'd pass 'em on their way back and forth to the store. After you got about a mile from the store there was a house and a farm on the side of the road about every half a mile.

I used to always look at the Seminole comin' through every day. That was the passenger train that run from Chicago to Jacksonville. It would come through every mornin' at around 10 o'clock. It come up over a long hill, and when it got up there it was goin' rather slow, so I could see inside the train, and could see the people in the dining cars. I could even see the silverware. And I used to think, "Well, them people must've come from where I really come from. Somebody must've threw me off the train here or somethin'. These people here are not my people. How did I get here?"

There were seven children in the family—three daughters and four boys. Four of 'em that lived, that is. One died when he was just a few weeks old. I was the second to the youngest. My father's name was Julius Martin. He never gave me nothin'. He worked hard, but he had a real mean streak in him, man. He could be very violent and sadistic. He always seemed to hate me—for what I don't know, but I guess he hated everything—the conditions of society and the life that he was trapped in. There was no way out of it for him, I guess he figured, and I reckon that's enough to make you frustrated. But he would unnecessarily beat me—just snatch me off the mule when he would come in from workin' in the fields and beat the hell out of me. And if he wasn't beatin' me he'd be beatin' on a mule or a dog. He never showed me any fatherly tenderness or consideration. He looked on me as somebody to work—to work and work and work. He made me pick cotton and hoe corn at a very early age. And if I wasn't workin', I was sleepin', 'cause that's all there was to do—work from sun to sun, then go home and hit the bed and sleep.

My mother was a beautiful woman—very Indian-lookin'. Her name

Painting by St. EOM depicting the village of Glen Alta, Georgia, as it looked during his childhood. Small figure at lower center is a self-portrait. Oil on linen, 15¾ x 18″ (inches), painted in New York City ca. 1938.

was Lydia Pearl. Story was her maiden name. Her father was a half-Indian. Creek or Cherokee. She had babies and took care of 'em, but she never did work in the fields. That's somethin' I never seen her do. I didn't worship her, but I thought she was a nice person, and I always felt kinda close to her. She was never overly affectionate with her children, but she was always kind and considerate of me. She would take up for me and show me a little sympathy sometime when my father would get too rough on me.

They always told me I was ugly as a child. But I don't think I was ugly. I *know* I wasn't, seein' some of the pictures I've seen. I had freckles, and I had cotton-top hair. I didn't cut my hair till I started school at six years old. I had to say a piece of poetry, and my father decided that I had to have my hair cut, like all the rest of 'em, to do it. So he cut my hair—just *forced* me.

My mother told me this years later, that just a few months after I was born my grandmother, Mother's mother, died, and left my mother two cows and some land to divide with her two brothers. And they sold the land and got 600 dollars apiece for it. And my father, like a big shot, he bought him a extra mule and rode up and down on the road, drunk, and hired a hand to do the work. And he pissed away that whole 600 dollars in just one year. And the crop was bad that year, too, my mother told me. But if my father had done pooled with my mother and worked with her, they could've got outta that trap they was in, cause she knew how to manage.

After they sold that land my mother inherited, they had no land. And we lived on this ex-slave plantation that belonged to a man named Sam Hatcher. He owned 5,000 acres, with quite a few houses and accommodations for the sharecroppers. He had two big old two-story plantation houses, one on each side of the railroad tracks. He lived in one, and the overseer lived in one. There was about two acres that was ours to farm. My father would go way off from the house sometime to plant potatoes, 'cause Old Man Hatcher didn't want you plantin' too much for yourself.

You didn't go to the store for food in them days—just for sugar and flour. Once a month when my father would get the 10 dollars that was his share of the crop, he'd go to Buena Vista in a wagon to get a few sacks of flour and some lard, if we were short of it—if the lard had done give out from hog-killin'. Or sometime he'd go down to the whorehouse and piss the 10 dollars away, and come back drunk, with maybe a dozen oranges. One time he brought a big grapefruit. We had never seen a grapefruit before.

But he'd get drunk, and he would sit in the corner, and I'd get the Sears and Roebuck catalog, and I'd ask him to get me things out of it, and he'd say "Yes, yes, yes," that he was gon' get 'em for me, but he never did. It was all a lotta shit. That was why I started to become suspicious of everything the older folks told me. They was always givin' me this crap about "You mustn't tell a lie," and "You must be honest." And then they'd tell you about Santy Claus and all that crap. And I got older, and I found out where Santy Claus was comin' from, and I found out where babies come from. It was a letdown to me, 'cause I thought, "Well, they been lyin' to me." It made me think, "Well, older folks is fulla shit." So I didn't ask them no more. If I wanted to know anything, I asked the black people that lived around Glen Alta. They would give you more of a straightforward answer.

In the summertime my father would say, "Well, we got these hogs we're gon' fatten. You pull the weeds and keep 'em fat, and I'll give you one in the fall, or I'll sell it and give you the money." But he never did that. He'd take it and piss it away, or we'd just kill the hogs for meat. So he was always a liar to me, and he always took a brutal approach with me. My sister told me that one time when I was about two years old, my father was holdin' me up by my feet and was fixin' to bust my brains out with a stick of stovewood, and she stopped him just in time. And I figured, "There must be some reason for him to hate me so dam' bad." So one time me and my mother was in the crib shuckin' corn, and I said, "I wanna ask you a question." I said, "Is that my real father?" And she didn't say doodle nor nay. She just took that ear of corn she was shuckin', and she hit me upside the head with it, and she got up and left.

My mother just got disgusted with my father, though. I remember one time when I was about five or six years old, it was wintertime, and it snowed. And I saw my father out behind the house with this neighbor woman, and he had her standin' up by this tree, fuckin' her. And I could see my mother lookin' outta the curtains from inside the house. That pissed her off. I guess my father had his charm, and he could use it when he wanted to, but he was very mean. Him and my mother always got to arguin' when it was time to plow the garden. See, my mother kep' the garden—hoed it and planted it and all. But my father had to plow it. And when it was time to plow the garden there would always be a big scene, because he didn't ever wanna do it the way she wanted it done. But it always wound up gettin' done the way she wanted it.

I don't think she ever loved him. She might've thought she did at first, but after she got onto his ways she just figured, "Well, I'm just stuck with this thing." 'Cause she didn't have nowhere else to go.

My mother and my father both of 'em grew up around Glen Alta, and we had family livin' all around. There was my mother's brother, Uncle Luther Story, who was a big, fat, pompous man. He was married and had about 14 children, made whiskey on the side, sold beef. Every once in a while he'd kill a cow and butcher it and sell it to the neighbors. But the people in the city got the inspection laws passed and stopped folks from doin' that. After that, you couldn't sell meat like that, 'cause it hadn't passed an inspection.

My father's father was always close around. At one time he lived up on this other place that Hatcher had, up there in Columbus where the country club and all that new subdivision is out in there now. He lived there and farmed for a while, and after he retired he come to live with us and help hoe and chop the cotton. I never did like him, because he always told me how sorry I was. And really I wasn't sorry. I worked and pulled the hoe just as fast as he did. But he was sayin' that, I guess, to work a psychology on me, to make me come on with it. But I always did my share, and I always thought, "I'm here. I'm not shirkin'. I'm doin' work and payin' for whatever I get, or what comes to the table." So I felt I had a right to dip in.

I only went to school six months out of the year, because the other times I had to be in the fields. I always had hard work to do—cotton pickin', choppin' cotton, and plowin' with mules, once I got big enough to stand behind a plow. When the cotton was all picked and the corn was pulled, I could go back to school. Then I'd have to drop out in the spring for the plowin', and school was over for me. Work, work, work—that's all I knew. Any spare time I had, I spent more or less in daydreaming—dreaming of the time when I could get away and escape all of this, because it held me like I was in a prison.

In school I would always draw on my tablet, and the teacher'd say, "Aw, you done drawed up your tablet, and now you don't have no room in it to do your 'rithmetic." You couldn't have nothin' else to draw on, except the blackboard, and you was only allowed up there for 'rithmetic. I was always dull on that. I didn't grasp it. I used to cry at the blackboard, 'cause I'd see them other kids workin' on those numbers, and I didn't know how to do it. But in readin' and writin' and history and geography and all that, I was the brightest kid in the class.

Comin' up in a little place like Glen Alta, I didn't have too much contact with the outside world. Sometimes down at the waitin' room I'd pick up the Chicago newspapers, and my mother would always buy the Atlanta paper on Sunday from the passenger train that went down to Americus. We didn't have no books in our house, except for my mother had one of these great big old thick Bibles. It was beautifully illustrated. That's what I used to go and find condolence in after my father would beat me. I'd go drag out this Bible and look at all these beautiful illustrations in there. They were by that Dürer. I didn't particularly care about the reading in the Bible, but I would look at the pictures and say to myself, "They're very good. I hope someday I can draw like that and be an artist."

I had an older sister who was about grown when I was still very young. She was 16 or 17 years old, and she adopted me under her wing. She'd take me with her when she went gawkin' around, lookin' for gossip and so forth and so on. She'd take me to this Doctor Hart's house. They had a piano, and she was learnin' to play it. We had had one, too, but it had gone back, 'cause we couldn't make the payments. But I learned to do the Turkey Trot at Dr. Hart's house, with my sister playin' the piano. Then they used to stay in Columbus in the summer sometime, and she'd go up there, and I'd go up there for a few days before she'd come back. And she'd take me to the theater. The stock company would be playin', and she'd take me to the drama. She kind of introduced me to culture, in a way, through that doctor's family. 'Cause they was a little more with it. Otherwise the people we went around was in the same boat we was in—sharecroppers.

I always looked forward to Saturday afternoon when I was a child. 'Cause on Saturday at this country store there in Glen Alta, down by the railroad tracks, black people would come from all directions and congregate there. And out among this group was a sawmill man named Will McGhee. He was a mulatto, they called him a Geechee. And he played the flute. Man, he could play that thing! He made it himself, out of a reed. And there was another black named Snap Chapman, who was a wedge hand over on the Brown place, and he could sand. He'd sprinkle sand on the floor of this old boxcar, which was fixed up like a waitin' room, there by the railroad track, and do like a soft-shoe in the sand. Sandin', they called it. And I had learned to do the buck-pat. So all these people would be standin' in the door watchin', and movin' about and comin' back and forth from the store. And Snap would dance, and Will would play the flute, and I would do the buck-pat for 'em. I really enjoyed those Saturday afternoons, because they took me away from the country life there. For this little bit, in this little place there, we was ourselves—jammin' and pattin' and dancin', and the flute was goin'. Man, it was really a good kick. The only other music I got to hear in them days was country guitars, but that didn't ever strike me too much. I knew it was music, but it didn't have much rhythm to it, and I liked that rhythm. Country music's for white people, and this was all black people down there at the store by the railroad. It wasn't no whites around most of the time, 'cept me.

I always liked to hang around black people's houses when I lived over at Glen Alta, and I played mostly with blacks. There was one or two of them black kids who could beat my ass, man, so I had to be nice to 'em. And I'm glad of it. It made me more congenial to get in there with them. I liked black folks 'cause they could laugh and talk. White folks around Glen Alta, in them days you hardly ever saw 'em laughin'. They was more uptight. And blacks wore more colorful clothes—red dresses and all such as that. That fascinated me, because I always had on just a blue shirt and overalls, or if it was Sunday and I went somewhere I had a white shirt and a short-pants suit to put on. But I loved the blacks for their colors. And black people knew that I didn't *talk*. I'd see and hear things at their houses, but I didn't run home and tell it. So they more or less trusted me. When somebody else white would come up, they'd flinch back. But they just kep' on natural with me when I would come along. It was from the blacks that I began to learn that you don't go 'round tellin' everything you know.

I always sympathized with black people when I was a kid. I guess it was because they was downtrodden and kicked under, and I had to work and toil in the fields same as they did. I worked with 'em when my father could hire one to help. I didn't mind it as much in the fields pickin' cotton or peas or flailin' beans or pullin' corn if there was a black person along, because they always had a rhythm about their bodies that I liked. In their work was a rhythm and a movement, a motion, that was like a dance. They laughed and played and sang, and would clap sometime, or shout a little bit, and sing songs. And you could talk with 'em about anything. The white folks didn't ever have no smiles on their faces, man. It was always a grim, determined look— determination about *what* I really don't know. I guess to get through life. They struggled to survive. But the blacks was even worse off, and that didn't stop them from havin' a good time.

Some of the older blacks who lived around Glen Alta were ex-slaves. There was Uncle Dick, who was run over when he was a little kid. But he was a *big* man, and he spoke with kind of a African twang. He'd been a slave for years, and he told me stories. I was always curious and inquisitive as a child, so I would ask questions about things. I'd ask some of them old black people, "How was it during slavery times?" And most of 'em said it was better. A few of 'em said it was worse, and some said it was about the same. But there was one who praised it highly. He had been what you call a *stud* on the farm, and he screwed all the young girls to get 'em pregnant, 'cause the master wanted to have fine big bucks like him to work in their fields. And that one also made bullwhips, which the master used to whip the slaves when they'd get outta line a little bit. He'd tie 'em up by the hands and whip 'em till the skin of their backs split, and then the whip boy would take salt water and pour it on their backs. But that old man still made fine bullwhips when I was comin' up, and he knew how to use 'em, too. He could split a small tree down with a whip, and things like that. He could hit a dime in the air with a whip. He was very adept at it.

My father didn't like blacks, and he didn't like for me to be around 'em. He used to beat my ass when I'd go off on Sunday to play marbles with the black kids. He'd say, "I told you not to play with them niggers!" And he'd beat the hell out of me, but I wouldn't cry or pout. I'd eat supper and take off my clothes and go to bed. One time my dog ran off after some slut in heat, and I found him down at these black people's house a little ways off. So I brought him home and took him down to the washpot. There were some suds in there, and I washed him and gave him a good bath. Then the next mornin' he come down to the field with me. The sun was just risin'—I can see it so vivid now—and I was plowin' the sweet potatoes. My little dog was layin' up on the furrow sleepin'. And my father comes out with the shotgun and he kills my little dog—just coldly kills him. And he says, "You ain't gonna have no dog that's been around no nigger!" So I just kep' on plowin', and I said to myself, "I hope he doesn't try to kill me." 'Cause he stood there with the gun, just lookin' at me, for quite a while.

There was one black guy who lived back over in the country near Glen Alta. He had a little land and a house, and he had a bunch of daughters. And they had kinda like a little whorehouse goin' over there. And the whites thought that guy shouldn't be lettin' his daughters sell their pussy like that. So my father and some of the other local farmers dressed up in sheets and pretended they was Ku Klux Klan—maybe they *was* Ku Klux Klan; I don't know—and they went over there and threatened 'em to stop 'em. They told him that when they got the crop in to get the hell outta there. So after they got the crop in, they moved out and went north.

Some of them white people liked to try to scare the blacks—to keep 'em in line, you understand. I remember one Saturday afternoon we was all down around the waitin' station there, singin' and dancin' and clappin'. I reckon I was about nine years old at the time. Will McGhee was playin' the flute, and people was comin' in for groceries—mostly just a little piece of side meat to cook greens with. And somebody said, "Look! Yonder comes a man up the railroad!" And I looked down the track, and there was a man with a striped blanket pulled over his head so you couldn't see his face, like he was tryin' to pretend like he was a ghost or somethin'. And I realized who it was. It was this man who run the store. 'Cause then I run to the store, and he wasn't there, so I come out and I thought, "Well, that's him."

Well, there was one black guy who had a shotgun, and he put it up on a forked stick, kneelin' on his knees. "If you come any further I'll kill ya," he says. So this guy with the blanket runs off down the tracks and into the woods. But there was a little boy there on the scene when that happened, and the next day he was playin' what he called "the game of dares" with his little sister. And he had got out his daddy's shotgun, and he dared his little sister, he said, "If you come any further, I'll shoot you," just like he'd seen that guy do. And his sister kep' comin' on, so he shot her and killed her.

They had a trial for him a few days later. It was my father, that man who run the store, and another man. They went down there, and they decided what to do with him. They decided they'd beat him with a rope. He was just about six or seven years old. He told me about it later. He said they got him and one of 'em helt onto his arms and another one helt onto his feet while the other one beat him—hit him several blows with that rope. That was his court trial. The authorities never knew about any of it, or if they did there was never nothin' said. But the guy that run that store had put that blanket over his head and come out there just to scare them niggers. There wasn't hardly no white people around there at the time. He was just tryin' to keep the fear of God in 'em.

I tried to stay outta trouble myself. I didn't lie or cheat or steal. Well, I would occasionally steal a few eggs from outta my mother's henhouse to go and buy some candy at the store. Or go and buy some tobacco to take to the convicts, who was in chains and livin' in a steel cage back down the road about two or three miles from Glen Alta. They were county prisoners, and this was down at Pineville at the time I'm talkin' about. But they went all over. This cage had wheels on it. They rode through this section and they'd be parked there, and then in the next few months they'd be parked in another section. And when they wouldn't be out there workin' with picks and shovels, they'd be locked up in that cage. They had to work from sun to sun, man, with them chains around their feet, and they didn't even take the chains off at night.

This was when I was around 12 or 13 years old. My father raised sugar cane, and I'd go to the patch and steal out 10 or 15 or 20 stalks and take it to them prisoners. I just felt close to 'em or somethin'. I knew that they was bad. There was some murderers there and so forth. A couple of 'em appealed to me, but I didn't know at the time what they was appealin' to me for. Now that I'm older I know that I was interested in 'em sexually. But I'd take 'em a plug of tobacco, or some sugar cane. And I'd pull up peanuts—a bunch here and a bunch there, so my father wouldn't miss 'em—and take those to 'em. Or pick 'em peaches and muscadines and things like that. 'Cause they didn't have a chance to get none of that.

There were some Gypsies that useta camp near Glen Alta, and I useta steal meat outta the smokehouse and take it to them, 'cause if I did that, they let me hang around. They dressed colorful, with the big full skirts and the gold earrings and bracelets and big scarves tied around their heads. They just fascinated the hell outta me. So I'd steal 'em a slab of meat, and they'd let me hang around, and I would listen to what they'd say, which was mostly in Gypsy language I couldn't understand. But when they read the cards and consulted people it was in English, and I would stand outside the tent where I could hear what they'd say. I didn't realize that I was gonna go into the same business later on, but many years later it all flashed back to me that I had been preparin' myself to be a reader all along.

I had a cousin who come down to Glen Alta not long before I left home. He wasn't my real cousin; my uncle married his mother, but they didn't stay together long. Anyway, his name was Carlton, and he was about 15 years old—a year or two older than me. He came down around cotton pickin' time and stayed for about three or four days, but he wouldn't pick cotton. He didn't like to work. He liked to ramble and roam, and he was tellin' me about goin' to New York with this guy who was in Vaudeville. He'd been around 42nd Street, and he told me about people who sold their bodies there. That didn't particularly impress me at the time, but I remembered it. He talked my father into lettin' us go into the cane patch, and we got some cane to chew on the wagon comin' home. And I remember we had an old piano scarf. The piano had gone back, 'cause we couldn't make the payments. But that night after we got back from the cane patch we got this scarf. It had tassels on it, and we'd take turns placing it around our heads, like a Madonna, and we'd look in the mirror and pose with it. This was all done in silence, 'cause otherwise the old folks would want to know what the hell you're doin'. We had an old oil lamp up on the dresser by the mirror, and he'd pose with the shawl and the bed, and I'd pose. I think I made the best poses. His weren't as graceful as mine. But the next day my father told him he had to leave. If he'd been a good cotton picker he could've stayed, but he wouldn't work. He would just sit in the cotton patch and watch us pick it.

The night after he left, I took that piano scarf and went outside to this plum bush thicket, and I gracefully placed this shawl around my head, and I knelt and faced to the full moon that was out that night, and I prayed to God to make me different from anyone else in the world. And by God, I think I succeeded in that prayer.

2. EARLY BLOOMER

Ever since I can remember I was interested in sex. It never seemed strange to me. I was *born* ready to go.

In fact, my earliest memories are of a little girl named Tessie, who seduced me at a very young age. I was about three years old. She suggested it to me, so naturally I obliged. That Tessie was a hot little baby! And from then on I had my nookie all along.

But Tessie died of pneumonia just a few years later, right before Christmas. And I remember vividly that Christmas Eve night when she lay there in her casket dead, and everybody was sayin', "Well, Tessie's gone to heaven now." But I wasn't thinkin' that. I was thinkin', "My God, what I've had is gone! Where'm I gon' find another one?"

Then came Boochie, a little black girl. She was a cute little thing, and bold as brass. I had gotten near 'bout seven years old, and she was the same age I was, but she was already fuckin'! She was fuckin' the local guys—two or three of 'em that liked little young chicks. Some of 'em wasn't that low down. They'd take an older girl. But one time Boochie even screwed my grandfather! And she always gave it to me, but I had to pay her a nickel. So the way I would get the nickel was I'd steal some of the eggs out of my mother's henhouse and sell 'em to get the nickel.

Well, in the meantime I had been busy breakin' the foreskin of my peter and skinnin' it back, which is somethin' all boys should do. They raise some of 'em to keep their hands out from under the covers, but I didn't. If I hadn't've skint it back it would've been an awful thing. Because I've seen men with foreskins that are really sad. You can't even pull 'em back, and that creates an odor, and sometime disease. So I pulled it back. I guess I was preparin' my penis for the work it had to do in the future. 'Cause there was gon' be quite a bit of it.

I remember one night one of my sisters come down from the room across the hall, where my mother and father was sleepin', and come in the room and got into the bed where I was. And she said, "Let's do like Mama and Papa. You can't make no baby." Well, I guess I was maybe 10 years old. She was older than I was, and she was always promiscuous. A real Miss-America-type baby. She threw her life away on a no-good tramp. She went into Columbus, and my brother was there boardin' with an aunt, and she fell right into the same circle that he was in. And she jazzed this boy and got pregnant. So my brother said, "You gotta marry him! You gotta marry him!" Which was the worst thing she coulda done. But anyway, it happened.

One time this boy I went to school with, I walked home with him to get the cows, and on the way we stopped to jack off. But I couldn't shoot my gun yet. *Oooo,* I was so pissed off! 'Cause he did it, and I couldn't. And I was *older* than him! He was 11, and I was 12. But I became more curious about masturbation, and I thought, "I got to get to see some of that come out!" So it wasn't long after that that I finally got a drop or two.

The last year I was at school in Glen Alta—I was 14 at the time—this girl came to teach at the school, and her name was Maude. And she was hot. She didn't fool with the students, but she did screw the man that ran the sawmill—Jonas Hancock, who was quite a character. Tall and good lookin', hung like a stud. In them days the teachers boarded with the families of the kids that went to their schools, and she boarded with his family. She boarded with us a little bit, but she didn't like it. It wasn't her style.

But anyway, this sawmill man rode an old mule, and when he would pass by the schoolhouse on the mule, that was her cue to go. So she would immediately get a headache and get sick and have to go home. And she would turn the classroom over to me, to hear the rest of the lessons and everything. I was the oldest kid, and the brightest one, except in arithmetic. But she had always done the 'rithmetic by then, so it was easy from there on out. All the answers to all the questions was in the back of the book.

So I'd hear all the other kids' lessons—there were only seven or eight kids in the class—and then I'd say, "Y'all go home now." And they'd all go home, all except these two little gals, Fanny and Nancy. They was sisters, and they were very bold. They'd both of 'em put it on the line. So naturally, as soon as the rest of the kids was gone from the class there was some fuckin' began. Right in the corner of the classroom, and on the seats, on the desks—everywhere! So we'd have a ball, and they'd go home. We just lived across the road from the school, so I couldn't stay long, because I had to go bring up the cows every afternoon.

Well, one afternoon Fanny and Nancy's brother caught me after school with 'em. So him and these two big cousins of his, they decided they were gon' drown me. But I didn't find that out till a few days later. I had a dog that had run off after some slut—this other dog—and I had found out where the dog was. He was at these black people's house that lived a little ways off. So I asked these three guys to walk down there with me, through the woods. And the more we kep' on gettin' through the woods and down toward this place, the more I got a feelin' of fear. Somethin' told me there was somethin' wrong there. So we got to where this deep hole of water was, and I heard one of 'em say to the other ones, "This is where we're gon' do it." So I thought, "Well, there ain't but one way to correct this." So I said to 'em, "Well, I'll lay down, and you can fuck me between the legs." Well, I spit on my hands, wet my thighs and pulled my legs together, and he got down there and fucked me between the legs and popped his rocks. And that seemed to compensate him. It had a psychological effect on him, I guess.

3. LEAVING HOME

quit school when I was 14 years old, 'cause I thought, "Well, if this is education, why pursue it any further?" And besides, I had always wanted to go off and leave the place, ever since I had got old enough to think. I had one ambition, and that was to leave, because I didn't see any future there for me. The things that I wanted to know and to seek and to enjoy in life just wasn't there. I thought, "Well, you better get the hell away from here, with all the things goin' on in your head, and the direction you wanna go." Man, I couldn't wait to get my first long suit and get outta there. Back in them days the police'd pick up a boy in knickers—a knee suit. So when my mother bought me my first long suit, I knew it was time for me to go. When I left, my mother said, "Don't you think you should ask your father?" I said, "No. What do I wanna ask him for? I'm gone."

So in 1922, I picked up my skirts and flew. I took off. And first I went to Columbus. I had a brother who was livin' there, and I went

118

to the house where he was boarding, and he took me in. So the next day I went ramblin' downtown. I was a curious child, and I was ready to embrace whatever crossed my path, or take any chance of any kind. And in downtown Columbus that day I met this guy who liked young boys, and he picked me up and took me out to the edge of town in the bushes and copped my joint. And then he gave me five dollars. So I didn't mind at all. Five dollars was a lotta money in those days. And I had on a long suit. I was searchin', searchin' for *anything*. I knew that there was some adventure out there, and if you found it and embraced it, it was your business to enjoy it. The spirit within your body causes such as that. It's no sin, and there's no reason to feel evil or guilty about it at all. I did have a kind of complex about this manliness stuff that they lay down on us, though. I thought that because I didn't think like the other men and boys that I knew, and 'cause I wasn't a violent person, it was wrong.

Well, this guy in Columbus gave me an address in Atlanta to go to. He knew a freak up there who liked young people, and I was streamlined, and had a nice build from all that toil in the fields. So I took the five dollars he gave me, and I hitchhiked to Atlanta and went to this freak's house up there. He worked in an office downtown. And he used me for a few nights. I didn't particularly care for him, but it gave me free lodgin's. So when I got ready to leave outta there, he gave me an address of somebody in Washington, D.C., and he gave me a couple of dollars. And I still had the five dollars that the guy in Columbus gave me. So I go on, then, hitchhikin' up to Washington. I was very lucky. I caught a ride all the way through. I didn't have to hit different towns.

But anyway, I got to Washington and I stayed there about two weeks. Made myself useful. Then after a while I said, "Well, I got to get to New York." And this guy in Washington happened to know somebody who lived in Trenton, New Jersey. So I took out, and I went to Trenton and stayed one night with this guy. He gave me coffee and breakfast in the mornin', and "goodbye and good luck." I went out to the highway and hitchhiked on up into Hoboken. And there I had to get across the ferry. I had done spent all the money I had, and this last guy didn't give me any, so I had to bum a nickel from a man to get across the ferry, and I got off down there in Lower Manhattan. And then I started to know the streets of New York— what went *on,* what went *down,* and what was *around.*

4. BRIGHT LIGHTS, BIG CITY

Before I went to New York I couldn't visualize a big city and bridges and waterfronts and such as that. I knew there was an ocean, and I had seen pictures in papers, but I was more just curious as to what was out there, and what I could encounter, and get through and make my expenses and live. I knew I had to make a buck to survive, and that survival was the key. You didn't ask how. Just survive. And in a big city like New York, if you're a nice-lookin' boy or a nice-lookin' girl, you can survive, if you don't make a bad reputation for yourself by roguishness and stealin'.

I went to New York with my eyes wide open and searchin' for other eyes. I had thrown myself on the mercy of the world. So the first night I was in the city I went to stand in Times Square. It seemed like I already knew where Times Square was, 'cause it drew me just like a magnet, man. I had heard of Times Square and 42nd Street from that cousin of mine, so I knew where I had to get to.

121

Well, you don't have to stand there long. There's a steady parade up and down, lookin' over the new crops that come into town. So this guy come up and said, "Where you from? I haven't seen you before." I said, "I'm from Georgia. I just got here." So he asked if I wanted to come along with him. His name was Hector Gonzalez, and he was a Spanish-speakin' guy from Colombia, South America. He looked like a kind person, and I knew I had to have a place to stay for the night. I didn't know nothin' about lookin' up rooms. They would've took all my money if I did. So I went home with this guy. He had a cold water flat on the Lower East Side, down on 23rd Street between Second and Third Avenue. He and I became very chummy, and I stayed with him off and on for about six years there.

Gonzalez was a cute little thing. He worked as a cook. He was brought to this country by somebody who sponsored him to get him in, and he had to work for those people for so many years before he could get his citizen's papers, and then he went on his own and got better jobs. They didn't pay him too well. Once he went off on a job up in New London, Connecticut, for about three months, and I stayed there and had the apartment to myself. I'd bring kids home that didn't have no place to sleep, but I just let 'em sleep there. I didn't fool with 'em, 'cause I never did go for young people. I wanted a man that was 40 or 50 years old. I have seen a few young ones—dam' few—that had that certain somethin' about 'em that turned me on.

Gonzalez had to go to work in the morning to cook the breakfast, cook the lunch and cook the dinner, so he wouldn't get back home till nine or ten o'clock at night. I had only been with him a couple of days when he gave me a key to his apartment. He said, "Here's a key. You can go and come." Well, that give me a chance, then, to venture off into the streets. So while he was at work I'd go hang around 23rd Street Park. I'd sit on the bench and watch people come by. So down there in this park I'd see these queens come by, and they all had bleached hair and wore Peaches & Cream powder—very pink and pale lookin'. And they didn't seem to be workin' or goin' to no job. Well, that appealed to me, 'cause I wasn't lookin' for no job. I was lookin' for somethin' where I could learn somethin'. 'Cause with this nine-to-five, man, there ain't much you can pick up. Not about life, anyway, and that's what I was interested in. If you don't get out and see it, you don't know about it. You got to rely on somebody's book to tell you about it.

So anyway, I met one of these bleached-blonde belles in the park there one day, and her name was Trixie O'Brien. She come up and said to me, "Hey, moll, where you from?" And I said, "I'm from Georgia." And we talked there for a little bit, then he said, "Well, come over to my flat for tea." She was a beautiful Irish queen. So I went over there and we had tea, and I found out why she didn't work: 'cause she had a Maltese husband who was keepin' her. A guy from the Isle of Malta. They're very much after boys there on Malta. The Moslem religion says, "Boys for pleasure and women for breeding purposes." All them Turkish countries is a buncha asshole bandits, man. So Trixie told me to come back over to her place the next day. She said, "Molly Malone and Dolly Wilson is comin' over, too, and we can talk." She wanted to show me off, see. So I come back over the next day and met them, and they was also queens who had Maltese husbands and didn't have to work. So I thought, "Shit, I'll have to get me a Maltese husband." So through them I began to meet some Maltese, and I learned to hustle them. You had to dye your hair blonde and use that Peaches & Cream powder, 'cause they wanted the more feminine type. And I'd live with one or another of these Maltese for two weeks, three weeks, sometime a month—that was about the longest. I'd find Gonzalez a good piece of ass—some boy who was willin' to be pliable—and I'd go off with one of these Maltese for a few weeks. I was around them a lot durin' my first year or two in New York.

One of them Maltese had a joke. He'd say, *"Hey, boy! Ya gotta place to sleep tonight?"* "No." *"Come with me. You'll sleep with me and my brother Nick."* And they'd get to bed, and the one that picked the guy up would say, *"Hey, boy! Take off your pants! Make more room in the bed!"*

But all durin' those years I was with Gonzalez, while he was at work I was learnin' about how to survive on the street and how to hustle. Sometime I'd go to 23rd Street Park and sometime I'd go to Times Square, and other places, too. And I learned very fast that some of these people that would pick you up would take you home and use you and put you out the door, and wouldn't even give you a piece of bread. So I thought, "Well, hell, I got to cope with this," and I began to demand money for my services. You couldn't make much money hustlin' them Maltese. They was all a dollar, maybe sometime two dollars. Didn't watch out, nothin'.

Gonzalez wasn't like me. He was one of these kind that wanted one lover, and I wasn't really lookin' for a lover. I was just lookin' for faces, to study 'em and to look at 'em and to learn the psychology of human nature. He didn't know about what I did durin' the daytime while he was at work, and he didn't like me goin' off with other people. He was jealous. So he would upset me sometime. That's why I got all these tattoos, man. I got 'em all durin' them first years in New York, when I was livin' with Gonzalez, 'cause he had told me I had a nice body and had said, "Don't never put no tattoos on your body." So when he'd upset me, like a dam' fool I'd go out and get a tattoo, just to spite him. One time I even thought about joinin' the circus as the tattooed man.

But when I could get away from Gonzalez sometime I'd catch the

Second Avenue el and go down to South Ferry or down to the Bowery or Chatham Square. That's close to Chinatown. They still had opium smokin' up on the high floors, up and down the stairs. Sometime I'd go in these bars down around Fulton Street and South Ferry, where these really tough seamen and all that shit hung out. I learned that was a good place to be around when the people was comin' back from work, if you wanted to be picked up. But a lotta them captains are wolves. Them were some tough people down there, and sometime I would get in fights there. That was back when I still thought I had to do shit like that to prove that I was a man. I still had a kinda complex about that. But one time I got shanghaied down there around South Ferry. This old wolf took a likin' to me, and he got me drunk, and he took me to his barge on Hiwanis Canal. He kept me a prisoner there for a while. But really I was kinda enjoyin' it. He told me, "If you leave here, I'll kill ya." But I just stayed till I got fed up, and then I left.

Then I got down in the Bowery and got strung out on them skid row characters down there. There was some real beauties livin' around there on the street, 'cause they was down on their luck and had done hit the rocks. Some of them was real interesting. They'd stay in 75-cent hotels down there, and their bodies were cheap. This was in '23, '24, '25, before I knew enough to venture out uptown. I would occasionally get picked up and get taken up there, but I had to learn how to dress and get aholt of some nice clothes before I started hustlin' uptown.

I was just gettin' used to the city. You get to the city, and it's a frightenin' thing if you let it frighten you. But I didn't ever let it frighten me. I was always too eager to see and live and learn and know what was goin' on in the city. That's what my ambition was. I had put my hands in the hand of God, and I said, "Wherever you lead me I will follow." So I began to meet all kinds of people. *All* kinds.

Over the years I was in New York I met 'em all. Actors, actresses, artists, dancers, faggots, lesbians, thieves, goofers, gangsters, politicians, pimps, whores—I met 'em all. From the highest to the lowest. I still prefer bums. They're more interestin'.

I was interested in the theatre when I first come to New York. But I began to get to know some of them actors, and they found out I wanted money for my body, and they give me the taboo then. So I really messed up there. If I'd just kep' on layin' with them and givin' 'em a little, first thing you know I would've got in a show or somethin'. They'd've thrown me a bone. But I was too independent for that. I didn't want nobody tellin' me when to go and when to come—"You got to be in at a certain hour," and all that shit. "You got to be at rehearsal," and all such as that. I knew how to keep a dollar in my pocket without havin' to put up with that, man.

I tried workin', but I didn't like it at all. These closet queens that useta run the employment office would get me a job sometime runnin' a elevator or somethin' like that. They was always on the lookout for green country boys, 'cause they could work 'em cheaper. I'd work a few days and I would quit. Some of 'em I wouldn't even go back for the pay, man. I just didn't like that. I wasn't learnin' nothin' there except how to run an elevator and stop it on the right floor. And it seemed like there was a hell of a lot more adventure and knowledge to be learned from hangin' out with the faggots downtown. They would always relate their experiences from the night before, and that was a lot more educational than operatin' a dam' elevator, man.

One night in around 1927 a guy picked me up, and he wanted to put me in a ballet school. He could tell, just from my walk, that I'd make a good dancer. He said, "You come with me, and I'll put you in a ballet school." Well, when I undressed and he saw all these tattoos, he fell out the window, and that was the end of that. So I realized that was gon' be a handicap, far as bein' a dancer went. But that line about wantin' to put me in a dancin' school could've just been bullshit from him, really. A lot of 'em who'd pick you up would tell you, "Oooo, I'm a movie director," and all that shit. I remember a few years later there was that one bitch who useta come down to Harlem every night with a greeeaaat big raccoon coat. He was "a movie director." He fooled me once, but he didn't fool me again. I went home with him, and he just had a three-room flat. So I thought, "Shit, you can't be taken in by a raccoon coat. You gotta be a better judge than that!"

So I began to learn.

The first couple of years I was in New York I didn't give much thought about home. I was out there in the world, and everything was unfoldin' in front of me. I didn't have time to think about home. I thought about my mother occasionally, but mostly the only thing I thought about it was I was so dam' glad to get away from there. I thought New York was paradise.

5. BUSTIN'

ein' gay was somethin' that wasn't talked about in the 1920s and '30s. The word "gay" wasn't even used then. But there was plenty of 'em that wasn't in the closet. There was screamin' loud faggots in the street. I didn't become one, but I associated with 'em. And occasionally I screamed and hollered and yelled, too. But they'd be walkin' down the street and see some bitch and holler, *"Wooo, Mary! Get her!"* You know, that would be some other bitch who didn't want nobody to know that they was gay. Well, they would just wanna fall right through the *street,* man! They wouldn't know whether to run, sit down, fly, or *what!* They just wished they could disappear from the scene. So I'd stop and talk with some of these screamin' queens, and I'd ask 'em who they was with last night, or what they did and what went on. And I'd hear all kinda weird, freaky things from 'em. They was always very open and frank about life. If they'd done somethin', they could tell it. They wouldn't do somethin' and then be ashamed

of it, like most people are. I feel sorry for them kinda people who're always ashamed and afraid of life.

For a while after I first got to New York I was confused in my mind 'bout whether I should be on the gay side or on the other side, and I had that complex about this manliness stuff they try to lay on you in this society. And for a long time it had give me a terrible complex the way they always said if you didn't go to school and didn't have an education, then you didn't know nothin'. But I got over them complexes later, when I decided it was all really just a matter of gettin' experience and knowin' people and knowin' things.

I was always lookin' for eyes, to search people out that wanted me. In the early days I had to learn them that would pay money from them that wouldn't, and all that. You had to learn to tell them there folks that just wanted to use you and then say, "Fuck you," and go on their business. You had to learn to steer around all of them, and to know 'em when you saw 'em. And some of them freaks would get you down a sidestreet and talk and talk and talk and talk and talk. And you'd just waste your fuckin' time. So you had to learn to tell all of that, and quick, too. You couldn't take no half a hour to do it. I learned to be very blunt. That worked very well. I useta pick up a lotta salesmen, and they'd say, "Man, you'd make a good salesman. You got so much gall!" I would seek out eyes, and I would say, "You want a good time?" But I would know they was out for somethin'. I could tell by the way they looked at me. That's where I started learnin' to be psychic. People could be walkin' behind me and I wouldn't even see 'em, and I could sense that somebody was on the make for me, and I would just walk around the corner, and they'd come around and follow me. They'd feel me up and so forth and so on. And I had to learn to put the proposition to 'em that I was outta work and I needed money. And I learned to get the thing over with and get my money and get on outta there. Unless I met somebody who had some money and wanted to go out to the clubs and wanted somebody to show 'em around. I'd take up time with them. That would usually be somebody from outta town. Salesman, executives, artists—you'd be surprised, man, at the people who're undercover. They come to New York and they let their hair down. They'd figure they was far away from home, and nobody would know nothin' about it.

You had to watch out for cops when you was hustlin' the street. You had to go home and change your clothes every time, and dress up in different pants and a different suit. 'Cause you wasn't supposed to loiter or walk up and down the street. They had dicks out there on the street to trap you. If you got picked up for hustlin' they'd send you to Rikers Island. I only got sent to Rikers once for hustlin'. Did 10 days. But I went there three or four other times for gettin' picked up in raids on joints that sold liquor. If you was picked up in a raid and you had money, you got out. If you didn't have no money, you'd go to Rikers Island for 10 to 15 days. Well, it didn't mean nothin' to me, 'cause I had nothin' to lose. I had my clothes on my back, maybe a shirt or two in the room, and a couple of pairs of socks. So what did I have to lose? Except my room?

But I had to learn who to leave alone and who not to fuck with, and so forth and so on. You had to always watch out for the ones that would shake down faggots in the subway or in office buildings, or anywhere. And these gangsters would come around and ask you, "When you're with a john, steal his identification and turn it over to us, and we'll put the shake on him." Well, I wouldn't ever do that. I had too much principle about myself.

One of the places where I hustled in them early days was Union Square. And at that time there was people makin' speeches and so forth there. All kinda things—revolution and yellin' in the street, or Jesus Christ messages. Long as you'd put up a flag and sit in front of it, you could say what you pleased. Or so they said. But I wasn't speakin'. I was just listenin'. I never did talk much in them days. I was pickin' up things. I was learnin' and listenin', 'cause I had a country hick voice, and I had to get rid of that and learn about speakin', and try to speak correctly, if possible. It was quite an ordeal, really, in a way.

So from Union Square I began to drift up to Bryant Park, between 41st and 42nd Street, right behind the New York Public Library on Fifth Avenue. I was always on the prowl. I'd go through the reading room and cast my eyes to see if there was anything. So I did research in the library, and then I'd go out and do research in the park. Bryant Park was where the hustlin' queens, the shakedown men and aspiring actors, lezzes and runaways and all such as that useta hang out. They always come to that center. Bryant Park wasn't well landscaped in them days. They had weeds growin' in certain parts of it, and sidewalks goin' through there into the bushes. The bitches turned many a trick back in them bushes. I never did, but I heard 'em say they did.

I had just started goin' up to Bryant Park in 1928, at about the same time the final breakup with Gonzalez come. He finally got fed up with my ways, and he put me out. Had a lock chain put on the door. So after he put me out I went up to Bryant Park, and I got to talkin' with one of these gutter queens. Her name was Tillie the Toiler. He had three dollars, and I had three dollars, and we both needed a place to live. So he said, "We'll put it together and go get a room." And by that night we'd done got a room on 63rd Street between Eighth Avenue and Broadway.

Tillie was the kinda person that liked to boss people around and tell 'em what to do. She liked to take charge of you and say, "Let's go rob a store," or somethin'. And he liked to give all the other gutter queens nicknames—Gloria Swanson, Greta Garbo, and so forth and so on. And they would hold christenin' ceremonies in the park when she was givin' out a new nickname. So they had this christenin' for me one day, and Tillie came up to me and said, "What kinda name do you want? Who do you wanna be like?" And I said, "I don't wanna be like nobody. I wanna be like myself." So I wouldn't accept nobody else's name. But Tillie hee-hawed around and said, "Well, you're tattooed, so we'll call you 'the Tattooed Countess.'" There was a book that come out around that time, I can't remember the name of it, but it had a character in it called the Tattooed Countess. It seems like it was by some Western writer. So anyway, from that time on I was called the Countess among the homosexuals. But among the goofers, the rough trade, I was called the Count, because I always had an aristocratic bearing and character and walk.

That Tillie the Toiler, I never did find out what his real name was, but he was from Providence, Rhode Island. And he was very vicious and mean, evil as hell, and he'd fight you at the drop of a hat, man. And I mean *fight!* After the first couple of weeks with him I realized that he and I couldn't get along. 'Cause he started jabbin' the needle. That was my first contact with junkies. He tried to talk me into shootin' it, but I wouldn't do none of it. I didn't know much about it at the time, but I had seen them addicts on the street. And them belles that lived with the Maltese had told me you could get hooked on the stuff. So at first he was just poppin' it—what you call "joy poppin'." You know—"I'm not hooked! I'm not hooked!" So he just did it about once a week for a while, and then come twice a week. And finally after a few weeks the rent come due, and I got a holt of my share, but he couldn't get his, 'cause he was spendin' all his money on that needle, and he was always hangin' around his connection. So I left him.

I did try that junk eventually, though. That wasn't long after I met Tillie. And it nearly killed me. I knew this Greek pimp that was on junk, and his whore talked me into takin' a shot. So I went over to their place, around 53rd Street and Ninth Avenue, and she give me a jab with that needle. But she give me too much. Well, about that time Tillie and this friend of his—a piece of trade—happened to come into this apartment. And Tillie said, "What you done to him?" 'Cause I was just sittin' there, man. That junk makes you oblivious to everything. But if Tillie and that friend of his hadn't took me outside, I would've o.d.'d. It had been snowin', and there was snow on the ground, so they walked me around out there and rubbed snow in my face to revive me. And I remember when I was startin' to come down, this pimp and his whore that had give me the heroin shot, they come by on the street. It was about two o'clock in the mornin', and he'd done beat her up. And he kicked her in the ass and said, "Get out and make me some money!" But anyway, I'm indebted to Tillie the Toiler for my life 'cause of that.

I almost tried that junk again, even after that. There was this bitch that rented out rooms in a buildin' on Sixth Avenue, and the junkies went there to meet their connections. So I went over there, and I was gon' make a connection. But when I went into the buildin' there was a mirror in the door, and all these junkies was goin' in and outta the place. They really looked pathetic, too. And I stopped to look in that mirror, and this voice said to me, "You wanna be like them?" And I turned around and walked away from there. I don't like nothin' that's habit-formin'.

But I always remained friends with Tillie. He would be in and out of jail, spasmodically. He'd be in two years and out maybe two months, and he was back in again. I would usually see him whenever I had to go to Rikers Island. He was always a pillar in the jail—one of the head knockers. He pushed junk in the prison for the racket people. And whenever he'd come outta prison I would always let him have a suit of clothes of mine, 'cause we was about the same size. But he finally died in jail, sometime around 1938, I think it was.

One of the places I would go to 'round the time I was livin' with

Tillie the Toiler was Saint Nick's Arena, on 66th Street between Broadway and Amsterdam. Sometime the civilians would get to fightin' the sailors in there, and all hell would break loose, man. They'd have rocks in their neckerchiefs and knock people in the head and throw people off balconies. Oh, man! Terrible!

You had to be careful, and really you had to be psychic just to sur*vive* in that scene, man. You had to know what was goin' on in front of you, behind you, and to both sides of you. You had to be hip to it *all*. You had to watch out for them gangs that come outta them rough neighborhoods. They'd come up the streets around Bryant Park and wanna beat up on all the faggots, and anybody else they could pick a fight with. So you had to learn to dodge them and to know when they was around. The word would fly, up and down the street, that so-and-so saw 'em headed this way. Well, you had to get off the street or else be fightin'. And whenever you rented a room you had to rent one you knew had a fire escape on top, where if them gangs come on through the house you could get on out over the roof.

You had to be on the watchout for these gangsters, too—these guys who was on the lam and had to stay off the street. They wanted boys, because whores talked too dam' much. So they'd come down in cars, man, and they'd see these swishy belles, and they'd pick 'em up at gunpoint. They'd say, "Get in!"

I went through all this shit, but dam' little of it thrilled me. Some did, but dam' little of it. It was just a duty to be done, to get the money and so forth and so on. All the time I was strivin' to find some way or some motive in my life, but nothin' seemed to motivate me any better at the time than this nightlife—runnin' in and outta night clubs and speakeasies down in basements. There was all kinda speakeasies where you could go in if you was known. The Village was the place in the late '20s. One I remember in particular was called The Black Cat. And there was one called The Hole. But some of 'em you had to pay before you went in, some you had to have a card, and some you could just walk in. But they was always bein' raided for sellin' liquor.

One reason the bright lights and the big city had drawn me in the first place was that I was kind of a stagestruck kid. I was always interested in the theatre—the opera, the dance, the musical comedy, the situation comedy. I was interested in all of that. And whenever these foreign groups—troupes from India, Czechoslovakia, Turkey, Africa, South America, Mexico—come into town, I always made it my business to get to the theater to see them and, if I could, get backstage, and meet 'em when they come out. There was always some gays in the group. Sometime you could get picked up that way. You had to put yourself where you could be seen by the right people.

So I was always lookin' for theatrical people. I was lookin' for any alley to get introduced to somebody that could pull me on, push me up or pick me up. And with them theatrical people I was able to learn more about speech. They was concerned about the enunciation of their voice, and I was interested in gettin' the Southern twang and drawl outta my head. Although it was always a compliment to me. It helped me, and a lotta people liked it, but I was tired of it. So I tried to seek out people with a little more goin' for 'em on the intellectual side. At first when I got to New York I didn't meet many intellectual people, except sometime somebody that picked me up when I got a chance to get away from that Gonzalez I was with. Otherwise I stayed on the outskirts. But later on I started meetin' people from Vaudeville, musical comedies—from everywhere. But them theatrical people all had a set routine, and I useta hear them curse and swear about how they were just sick of the theatre, and goin' up there and doin' them same performances night after night after night. And I thought to myself, "Well, shit, that's just the same as slavery, or goin' to a job." So then I began to lose interest in it. I had opportunities, but I didn't pursue 'em, 'cause to me the street and life was the most interestin' thing of all. Bein' in there as an actor, well, you got a chance to act, but you couldn't always be yourself.

Durin' all this time the drag balls was very popular, and there was always the thrill of goin' to the drags. All the elite went in the theatrical world, the writers' world—all kinda people, racketeers and everything. I always won the prize for most original. I never won the first prize for beauty, but for most original. One night I went with just a G-string on. I was nekkid except for that and a big Bird-of-Paradise headdress from Hawaii—the real thing. And that was all I had on, and a gilded body. I was painted gold from head to foot, man. And the dam' cops wouldn't let me in. They said, "Well, you can stay, but you have to stay back here in this closet till the inspectors have come and gone." So they put me in this fuckin' closet, man. And I had to set there till 11:30. Then they let me out on the floor. The celebrities was there—Tallulah Bankhead and Clive Brooks and many others. Some of the Whitneys and the Vanderbilts was there.

So that was the diversion. You was hustlin' all the time, and you were lookin' forward to the next drag. So no sooner than you'd get one drag costume planned and made than it was time to start plannin' on another. The rest of 'em either bought evening gowns or costumes with big feathers on 'em and so forth and so on, but I always designed and made my own. There would be hundreds of people at them drags, man. Thousands! In fact, they even rented Madison Square Garden and had one. Most of the time they had 'em at Rockland Palace, I think it was called, on 153rd Street.

I knew a lotta chorus boys in New York, and I had a chance to go to chorus call once myself, but I decided not to go. I don't know whether I would've been picked or not, 'cause I always had a rhythm of my own. I shivered and shaked long before Elvis Presley come on the scene, man, but they said I was vulgar, and they'd put me offa dance floors when I'd go to dances. They'd say, "You're vulgar! Get off!" 'Cause I wanted to let the girl stand in front of me and wiggle and all such as that. I always felt like I had some kinda black rhythm in my body. Later on I started goin' to them tribal films at the Museum of Natural History, and I'd sit in there for hours, just seein' 'em over and over, because they fascinated me. The way them people walk, the natural gait—that's hard to acquire when you're comin' up in a rigid, conservative society. But I had that rhythm ever since I was a boy, because I was always with these black people who would dance and do the buck-pat.

But all they ever paid them chorus boys was 50 dollars a week, and I was makin' far more than that—about 150 dollars a week. And I was havin' a free life besides—runnin' all over town, doin' the clubs, pickin' up people, meetin' people. But them chorus boys would be in there doin' rehearsal all day, exhausted, and be havin' to rest to get back the next day. 'Cause they worked the shit out of 'em, man. I used to see 'em come home. So I thought, "Shit, that ain't for me. I wanna see life. I don't wanna see out over the footlights."

So I stuck to the hustlin', and I kept learnin', pickin' up things. For the first six years I lived in New York I never left. After the breakup with Gonzalez and after I left that Tillie the Toiler, I lived by myself for a while. I went and got me a room for three dollars a week—just a hallway room without a window, and a room with a stove nearby, so you could cook a meal there. That was near Campbell's Funeral Home, where they useta lay out all the celebrities. Valentino lay there in state, but I didn't go see him. He wasn't my type. I didn't go for them greasy-haired types, man. They was evil.

After I got that room by myself, Tillie the Toiler still come over and slep' on the floor. So I decided, to get him away from around my neck, I'd just come home—go back to Georgia for a while. That was in the fall of 1928. My mother needed help gatherin' the crop, 'cause my father had just died a few weeks before that. Just dropped dead one day all of a sudden after he'd done drove the wagon to Buena Vista.

6. THE FARM & THE FACTORY & THE CRASH

After the first couple of years I was in New York I had started writin' to my mother occasionally, but I hadn't really thought about goin' back home, because I had no desire to communicate with my father or see him. I hadn't got over that evil, domineering attitude that he had showed toward me when I was a kid. So when he died I felt a great freedom of release, 'cause there was never any love between us.

So after he died, in the fall of '28, I come home for the first time in six years to see my mother. She wasn't livin' at Glen Alta no more. She was livin' in this house here, which she had saved the money to buy her own self. She had a couple of cows that she had got from my grandmother, and those cows began to multiply. And she started savin' a little money by sellin' the cream from the cows. She didn't ever let my father get his hands on it. She kep' it under her control, and she finally saved up enough to make a down payment on this place where I live now. It was right after my father died. Old Man

Hatcher, who owned the house they was livin' in at Glen Alta, he found out my father sold a bale of cotton that he wasn't supposed to sell. So he told my father to get off the place. Well, by then my mother had done saved 500 dollars, so she took it and paid it down on 374 acres and this house. And my father went to town to get the mules—he had his own mules to hitch up to his own wagon—and he dropped dead. He was just about 45 years old. So my mother took it from there. And I come home that fall. This was just an old farmhouse then.

Well, anyway, from 1928 on I began to come home every year and help with the crop. That way I could escape the turmoils of the city. Not that I liked it down here, but I knew the corn had to be pulled and the cotton had to be brought in. I felt out of tune here, though, and out of harmony, and I knew that it wasn't what I wished and what I wanted, and it wasn't the kinda life that I wanted to see and learn about. So I looked at it this way: "I'm here. I know it. Go on and do it. It's got to be done—the cotton to pick, the corn to gather, the wood to be got, and so forth." I always paid my way by workin'. And when I'd come here I'd just fall right in with the rest of 'em, and I was just like them. I'd go to the field and plow or pick cotton, pull corn or pick peas. And I didn't try to put no shit on with nobody. They only knew what I told 'em 'bout what I did in New York, and I didn't tell 'em much. They did wonder about how I got all them beautiful clothes, though. I'd come down here with this gay wardrobe—clothes I'd done hustled or made—and I'd give 'em away to my cousins and all before I'd go back to New York. They'd say, "Where'd you get all these clothes?" And I'd say, "I worked for 'em." They never did ask me what I did, and I didn't tell 'em. They had a idea of what I was doin', though, 'cause I was swishy in front of 'em—"*Ooooo, Mary!*" and all such as that. But they couldn't figure me out, 'cause I was a different character.

I eventually told my mother that I was gay. We was out there washin' the clothes under that pecan tree, and I told her that I liked men. And she said, "Well, you're still my son. I love you, whatever you are." She didn't say no more about it. She was very understanding. My mother was a broad-minded woman. Sometimes she'd get fed up with me, though. When there was work to be done, I was very welcome here. When there wasn't much work to do, we'd fall out. I'd sit around and read Western stories, and sometime I'd draw a little bit—just pass the time. There wasn't no radio or nothin'. But she'd get fed up with me and tell me to get out. So I'd just grab my bags and hit the highway and hitchhike back to New York.

I remember one time I was down here, it was just a few years after I'd started comin' back again, and these guys was gonna lynch this black man, and they asked me to come along. A girl I had went to school with was married, and she and her husband lived up by the highway. And this black guy escaped from the chain gang, and they said he raped her, and they caught him. My cousin come by and he said, "We gonna lynch that nigger tonight. You wanna go along?" And I said, "*Noooo!* I don't wanna go to no such as that." I said, "That person ain't done nothin' to me. I don't wanna be bothered." So I went to sleep. And he come back way on into the next mornin' and was tellin' how they'd taken knives and cut this guy's penis off and split his balls off and slit back his skin. He was still *alive*, now, and they were doin' this to him! And finally one of the guys—I reckon he must've gotten merciful—shot him, right in the forehead, and killed him. Well, that one that shot him was a sawyer in a sawmill, and a year later to the day a sliver slipped from a log he was cuttin' and hit him right in that same spot on his forehead and killed him, the way he shot the bullet in that guy.

But that first time I went back home, in '28, after I'd been down here for a few weeks, that Gonzalez sent me some money to come back to New York and take a job cleanin' this Jewish doctor's office—75 dollars a month, and I could live there, and he'd feed me and all. Gonzalez was workin' for him as a cook at the time. Well, this doctor had all these fuckin' instruments, man—all kinda machines to cure you of cancer or some kinda shit. And I was supposed to go down there every mornin' and polish it all over and make it all smooth-lookin'. But I'd go down there and set back in the corner and go to sleep 'bout half the time.

All the servants were s'posed to be in the gate at a certain hour, but I got to stayin' out late at night. One night I come in late, and I come right in through the main lobby and come up on the elevator and come through the drawin' room. I was drunk, and I had a serape, or a Spanish shawl with a pin, and I throwed it around my shoulders and did a Spanish flamenco dance, man, and swep' on back. And Hector told me, "You can't do that! You can't do that! You got to be here and do this and do that and do that!" So I just said, "Well, fuck this," and I quit.

Well, about that time my brother had done went to Michigan and got a job in an automobile factory. There was a foreman up there who was from this part of the country, and he knew us. His name was Ralph Guy. And he said, "Come on up and you'll get a job." So I took a guy who was livin' with Gonzalez—I can't remember his name—and we took a bus and went out to Pontiac, and I went to work in the factory. That was in about February of '29. First I went in pushin' these carts from one track to another, then I got over into the oil sandin', which is very backbreakin', man. Well, Ralph Guy was workin' in Detroit at the Fisher Body plant, where they make Buick bodies. And he come over to Pontiac, and he said he could get me a better job over there. He liked me. He wanted to have an affair, but he didn't appeal to me. I did go from Pontiac over to Detroit, though, and got a job at Fisher Body Works. The money was pretty good. You could make 12 or 14 dollars a day. But I laid out a lot.

So I worked and made a little money and cruised around. And then in September or October the Crash come. We just went home from work and come back the next mornin', and the dam' place was closed. I read in the papers that the stock market had crashed, but what the hell did I know about the stock market? When I left the front gate at Fisher Body plant that mornin', I didn't see any of them people I worked with no more. I packed my clothes and took the bus back to Georgia. I had about 70 dollars. And I thought, "Well, shit, I got to go home and hustle on that farm—pull that corn and pick cotton. I might as well have a little fling first." So I stopped in Atlanta and stayed till Halloween was over. I stayed with my sister Kate. She lived in College Park, right on the outskirts south of town. Her husband took me to a beer joint and had 'em put some knockout shit in me. He didn't want me there in his place, but I thought, "Shit, it's my sister. She's always entertainin' his brothers and sisters." They had two boys, and I'd set up at night with the two of them. I guess he put two and two together.

But I met a queen in Atlanta who worked for the government in the post office, and we became friends. He had a car, and I was good-lookin', and could always track somewhere he couldn't. He liked me, too. I reckon he thought I might make a pass at him, but he didn't appeal to me. He made himself convenient every night with his car. I spent most of my money on cloth, stuff to get up my costume for the drag, and the wig and everything. In Atlanta on Halloween even in them days you could get in women's clothes and go out in the street, and they couldn't do nothin' about it. So we dressed up in drag and went out in the street, and we went to some Halloween parties. And then after Halloween I hitchhiked on down here to help harvest the crop, and I stayed till February of '30. I had done been gone from New York for a whole year. That was about the longest I was away from there till I left for good in '57 to come back to Georgia. But it was good to be back in New York. That was where you could get a good, liberal education. If you were willin' to pay the price.

7. HIGHS & LOWS ON THE STREET & ON THE ROAD

When I got back to New York that winter I wound up in Bryant Park again, and I run into Tillie the Toiler. He was still on the scene. He wasn't in jail at that time, and he had a room. He wasn't hustlin' then, he was stealin'. He was a booster—a shoplifter. So he gave me the key to his room, and that night I was at the automat on Sixth Avenue— Avenue of the Americas—near 42nd Street, and I bumped into this gay kid that I had met when I was in Detroit. His name was Clarence Hogue, but I called him Miss Detroit. I had met him at this General Motors executive's apartment. And he said, "Well, let's get a place together." Tillie was on the needle at the time, so I didn't wanna stay with him. So Miss Detroit and me got a place on Eighth Avenue between 46th and 47th Street. Some kinda hip place was downstairs, where the showfolks ate. It had kind of a campy name, but I can't remember it right now.

I was in and outta New York all durin' the early '30s. I lived there with Miss Detroit for a while, and I lived with some of the other hustlers durin' that time. There was one named Betty Boop, who was a little bitty, short faggot from Long Island. His real name was Jimmy Lyons. I lived with him, but not for too long. And there was Stella Dallas, who I also lived with for a while, and then later on there was Leo Elmore.

Stella Dallas was one of the queens I had met a few years before in Bryant Park. She'd been at that first christenin' I went to there, when Tillie the Toiler gave out the names. He had a guy keepin' him at the time, too. All he did was run up and down the street hollerin', *"Oooo, Mary! Get her!"* and all such shit as that, with his elegant clothes and his hats and his Florsheim shoes. He was the height of fashion, and screamin'. Later that john put him down, then he had to go hustle hisself, but when I moved in with him he had this old auntie who was keepin' him. She worked on Wall Street and had gotten him a job down there, too. He worked in the mail department, or so he said, at one of them there stockbrokers. Stella Dallas had quite a few Wall Street johns on a string for quite a while, but he wasn't too much at pickin' up. He always tried to be too fuckin' ritzy. The ones that picked you up on the street didn't like it if you were too ritzy-lookin'. They'd rather have you a little seedy-lookin', 'cause they'd figure you knew less and they could get you cheaper.

Stella Dallas was the one who taught me to hustle the west side of Fifth Avenue. He said, "Go over there. You'll meet a nicer class of man. You won't get all these Greeks and Maltese and Italians or whatever." So I went over there and I asked for more money, and I got it. So I thought, "Shit. Fuck 42nd Street." When I went through there I was just lookin' over the passin' parade. 'Cause I have never got a good john offa 42nd Street. Some of 'em made some good scores there, though. Some of your actors today made their scores on 42nd Street—your directors and so forth, and people who introduced 'em to the theatre. You always saw them in the street. That was the theatrical district, and they wasn't too hinkty about who rented a room, and they was kinda bohemian and minded their own business. They were more liberal, more tolerant.

The hustlin' area was from 59th Street down to 42nd. But on Fifth Avenue they come out from that theatre district, and the first side they came to was the west side, so they went up it. Just before and right at theatre time was the good cruisin' on the Avenue. And there would be all kinda gay people hustlin'. There was me and Stella Dallas, Bobby Mirror—he was from Boston—and Greta Garbo, Miss Jersey— he was a chorus boy. He was in "The Student Prince," and I think he was in "The Merry Malones," too. But he later got hooked on the needle.

Anyway, if you wanted to hustle the Avenue you had to be quick with your speech, intelligent, and had to know about culture, 'bout theatre and so forth, 'cause most of that was in the air. Most of the people had been to the theatre, and they'd make the pickup on the way home, if they saw somethin' they liked. They generally wasn't the type of people who particularly went out cruisin' every day and every night. They were what you call "closet belles." And, aw, God, you'd be surprised at the walk of life that they come from. From the richest people—businessmen, senators, congressmen, governors—all the way down. I met all kinda people, man. And you had to cater to their desires. There was a judge one time who wanted to beat people with a stick. I was willin' to go, but he wouldn't take me, 'cause I was bigger than he was, and he was scared I might turn on him.

I lived for several months up in the 60s, off Central Park West. Miss Detroit and me lived up there for a while, and later I lived with Stella Dallas in that same neighborhood. But I didn't like that neighborhood. I felt more at home down there in that theatrical district, where you knew who was faggots and lezzes and whores and pimps and thieves, and everything was out there in the street. You didn't see that up there in the 60s. In the theatrical district you could scream a little and they wouldn't put you out, as long as you paid your rent and didn't cause them no trouble.

So Stella Dallas and me moved outta that place up in the 60s and into this hotel down on West 47th Street. And in this hotel was all kinda whores and pimps, and I really felt that was my atmosphere. Other times I had appeared in the streets, and I hadn't felt that I had reached my niche. But when I got in there and saw all these people, all these different kinda people, communicatin' and dancin' and havin' a good time, I felt, "Well, this is where I'm lookin' for. This is life. You can see people, see their expressions, their reactions and so forth and so on."

Well, there was a couple of flim-flam artists in this hotel. The guy was a flim-flam artist, and the bitch he lived with, when she wasn't flim-flammin', she was hustlin'. And they smoked opium. Stella Dallas knew them, and he took me over to their room. They was down there puffin' on that opium pipe, and they had the room fixed up for it. There was sheets all wet all over the bathroom, hangin' down over the windows, where the scent couldn't get out into the hall so strong. So they wanted to give me a puff. Well, I didn't even smoke cigarettes. Although I tried 'em, but they didn't appeal to me. Anyway, I tried to puff on that pipe, but I couldn't. And they said, "Well, you can't puff the pipe, so we'll give you some *yinchi*." That's the ashes of the opium after it's been cooked, and you can put that in coffee and drink it. So they put some of that in a cup of coffee, and I drank it. I didn't go into no great fantasy or no ethereal world. Life was about the same, only I felt contented. And I began to think to myself, "All this shit you been believin' about you can't do nothin' because you don't have an education is a lotta shit." So I thought, "Well, out here in the street I'm gonna learn from this life."

I lived with Stella Dallas for four or five months, until he went to Ohio and got picked up for passin' counterfeit money and got throwed in jail. That was in the fall of 1931, 'round Thanksgivin' time. That's when I got a place with this guy Leo Elmore, who said he'd had a swank apartment on the East Side, and he'd been makin' pretty good money, but he'd lost his job, so he had to move out. He had been a ticket snatcher at the Paramount Theater, and he was rippin' off a little and got caught, so they fired him. Well, me and Leo pooled our resources and got a room there on 56th Street, in a place where they also rented rooms to hustlers to hustle tricks in.

In the same buildin' there lived two French prostitutes called Sonia and Eva. They had French pimps, and every night when they made their money they had to go to the Western Union office and send their earnings to France—what they didn't hold back. And they helt back quite a bit. One of 'em took me up to her room one night for the trick. She charmed me in, and she come on the attack. She said, *"Eddie! Eddie! Come on!"* I paid for it, but it didn't turn me on. And she opened her trunk and flashed a big fuckin' roll of money. Well, she was hot for me, because she useta say, *"You make me hot, Eddie!"* And I never did pick up on it. She had bad ankles. Thick ankles. If I ever go with a woman, she's got to be *per*fect from head to foot. And all of 'em ain't that way. Not by a long shot.

Well, that was right offa Fifth Avenue, and I lived there with Leo for 'bout 18 months. And he got in touch with a German whore, Marcel, across the alleyway, and he got to fuckin' her, and he was hustlin' too. In those days I had a routine. I always hustled the Avenue from nine till twelve every night. I did it religiously. And of course anywhere I went, daytime or nighttime, I always had my eyes open, lookin' to see if there was anything.

I lived with Leo from around the end of '31 on into the summer of '33, when the two of us decided we would go to Chicago to get a job at the World's Fair. So we caught the bus and went there and got a room, but we didn't get no job at the World's Fair. We tried to hustle around and make a few bucks on the side, but the hustlin' wasn't too good in Chicago. Nobody wanted to pay more than a dollar or two dollars, and they was dam' few and far apart.

Well, in Chicago we got in with these two campy queens, Jack Curtis and Howard Carney. They'd been hustlin' there—existin', which was about all any of us was doin'. But they had done a lotta freight train ridin', hoboin', and they told us all about California and how easy it was to get by out there. I didn't know it then, but what they called "gettin' by" was layin' on somebody's floor and sleepin'. But anyway, they said, "Oh, come on! Let's go to the West Coast!" So we decided we'd go catch the freight and go out to California on it.

So we caught us a boxcar there at the Burlington Railroad yard in Chicago, and we went through Omaha and Denver, Salt Lake City, Sacramento, and on into Los Angeles. We'd stop for a day or two in some of them towns. We had no money, and I got hungrier and hungrier, so I had to learn about goin' to people's back doors and beggin' for food in these towns along the way. At first that was hard for me to do, but I become used to it, and I met some nice people who gave me some of whatever they had to eat. And sometime I'd go down the street and panhandle. I'd ask for a nickel or a dime or a quarter. That song about "Buddy, Can You Spare a Dime?" come out around that time.

We rode the train all through that desert country out West, which I had never seen before. It was really beautiful, man. Sometime the train would stop out there in the middle of the desert, and Jack Curtis would get off and stand out in the desert doin' dramatic scenes. I would say, "Do somethin' tragic for us." And he'd moan and perform while the train would be stopped in the desert there. One time he was out there puttin' on a show, and he run up on a rattlesnake. And one time, like fools, we got on the wrong train out there—one of these fuckin' desert locals. And we got off in this orange grove and went out gatherin' oranges, a whole bunch of 'em, and we got to throwin' 'em at one another up on top of the train, which was a bad thing to do. We put 'em inside our shirts and was up there while the train was ridin' along, and was throwin' 'em—at each other and at people the train would pass, too. So when we got to the next town they had the cops there and took us off and told us to get outta town. That was some little town outside of Sacramento.

But we finally made it on into Los Angeles, and we got a room for three dollars a week. Jack Curtis and Howard Carney introduced us to the cruisin' areas out there. The room we got was near Pershing Square, which was one of 'em. The other main one was Westlake Park, not too far from Hollywood. It was a congregatin' place for hustlers and whores and pimps and bums and everything. And them folks'd come rollin' up in them great big old cars and expect you to get up and just be at their pleasure. It would've been all right if it was somethin' you wanted, but there wasn't hardly none of 'em that I wanted. I did meet one director there who took me up on the mountaintop high, and he wasn't too bad. I liked him. But the others were bastards. Them actors and extras and all of that was always comin' around and bullshittin' you, and tryin' to get you for nothin' and all such as that. Leo had better luck out there hustlin' than I did. He could get thrilled by them characters, but I couldn't.

I did get introduced to pot for the first time out there, by a guy I met in Westlake Park. In those days you could buy it all cleaned and manicured. It didn't have no seeds or stems in it. Or you could buy rolled joints. I reckon the first time I ever saw pot was in Bryant Park in New York. There was this bitch named Peggy O'Neal who would come there every night with a cigar box fulla rolled joints and sell out and be gone, man. She finally got caught and did time for it. But I had never smoked any of it until this time in Los Angeles in '33. And at first I couldn't get any kick out of it. I didn't get high on it the first time till later on.

Me and Leo only stayed in California for about 10 days. That Los Angeles was a very cheap town, man. In New York I knew where everything was, and money was better. So we left Jack Curtis and Howard Carney out there and caught the Southern Pacific and started back to New York. I remember in El Paso, Texas, I tried pot for the second time. Me and Leo bought a Prince Albert can full of it from a Mexican kid down by the freight yard there, and I tried to smoke some of it, but I still didn't get high. I couldn't ingest the smoke.

I made several more trips back and forth between New York and California in '33 and '34, but I never did stay out there on the West Coast for long. I did finally learn to ingest that marijuana smoke when I was out in Los Angeles on one of them later trips. I got holt of some pretty strong stuff out there. It was prob'ly from Mexico. And I puffed that a little bit, and I learned to get a glass of water, and get a mouthful of smoke and drink the water to hold it down. And when I started doin' that I began to get a buzz. And all of my inhibitions and complexes and so forth left me.

Before I began to smoke pot and learned to hold it down and get high, I thought things I had done and had been doin' was wrong, and was a sin. And you'd die and go to hell, and all such as this. And I'd had this complex about "Well, you didn't go to college, so you can't do nothin', and there's nothin' for you to do. You just got to be what you call a 'peasant.'" But when I began to smoke pot I began to realize my potential. I could see myself in a truer light. Pot opened up my mind and helped me realize that whatever you wanna be in life, you can be, if you're determined to see it through. Pot broke down all my inhibitions, and I began to believe in myself.

When I went out into the world I was lookin' to see what was what, and I saw that there was whiskey-heads, winos, canned-heat freaks and junkies and opium smokers, and I knew there was weed-smokers. So I looked 'em over and I thought, "Well, the weed seems to hold up the best and keep the self goin'." And then when I discovered weed, and got that first buzz off it there in Los Angeles in 1933, I thought, "Well, shit! This is what you left home for!"

8. A WHOLE NEW WORLD

)made my last trip out to California in 1934 with Mona Brown. He was from Birmingham, and was tryin' to be a writer. He wrote me a letter and says, "We'll go and take our farewell tour," like it was some great actress sayin', "This is my last tour." But he woulda made a good writer. He wrote a article that he was tryin' to get published about Joe Huddleston—a campy queen from Birmingham, like he was, who went to New York and got in a play with Mae West. They raided that, closed it. And then Huddleston went back home to Birmingham and run his mother and father outta the house with a butcher knife, and they had him put in the insane asylum. He stayed in there for a few years, and then he got out and finally went to teachin' school. Or so I hear, now. That's what Mona told me.

So anyway, we took our farewell tour. We come down through the Southern route, hitchhikin', and stopped off there in Birmingham, and was in Alabama a few days. One night we went up to Gadsden, where this belle lived that Mona Brown knew. She lived with her brother. So we went up there and then all of us went out to this roller rink there, and I started gettin' a bad viberation there, man. Mona Brown always went for these types that would stir things up and get you in trouble, so after we was at this roller rink for a little while one of them, or both of 'em, started passin' the word around that a bitch was there and wanted to go out. And I started to feel that bad viberation in that place, man—I had just started to develop my psyche and pick things up like that—and I said, "Let's get the hell outta here!" And 'bout that time I heard somebody say, "There's a buncha cocksuckers here!" Man, they sounded like they was ready to lynch somebody. We got out before the chase began and took off runnin'—through people's yards and down these sidestreets and jumpin' over fences. They didn't catch us, but Mona Brown ran into a line of barb wire and cut a big gash over his eye. He was lucky it didn't put his eye out. But he had to go to the hospital and get that gash sewed up.

So we got outta Alabama and went on through Memphis, Little Rock, Oklahoma City. And in Oklahoma the farmers and the local deputies would come out to the freight train and round up anybody they found on the boxcars. They'd have guns and take you in to some kangaroo court, and you'd get sentenced to work on these pea farms for nothin', 'cause the farmers was in with them deputies. This was goin' on around McAlister, Oklahoma, and we'd heard about it, so we jumped off when the train was slowin' down before it got into the freight yard, and they didn't get us.

There was a lotta people ridin' the freight trains in them days. After we got outta Oklahoma City and were comin' through to Amarillo we were on this boxcar with 40 or 50 people on it. And there were these two young girls on there who was gang-fucked by quite a few of 'em. It was nighttime, and a lotta people were sleepin', or tryin' to, and I couldn't see what was goin' on, but I could hear them two girls back there sayin', "Don't hurt me! Don't hurt me!" And Mona Brown was tryin' to fool around with this guy in there while all that was goin' on. It was all squares in there, man, and they didn't like that. I had to hit one guy, 'cause several of 'em was comin' at us. The train was slowin' down as we come in closer to Amarillo, so we just jumped off the train then and took out through the prairie land. We had to walk about six miles into town.

Well, from Amarillo we was gon' catch over to Albuquerque, New Mexico. But they stopped the train in Vega, Texas, and threw us off. We was the only two on the train, and the brakeman pulled a gun out and said, "Get outta here." So we got off the train, and about that time a big dust storm come up, man—a tornado and a dust storm together, 'cause we could see the tornado. And we ducked into this store. We had about 15 cents, so we bought some bread and about a nickel's worth of baloney. So we was in the store, and the grocery guy had a bucket there, and Mona turns this bucket upside down and sets on it. And I see this grocery guy gives us a dirty look. And he had a pistol on his hip. So I said, "Man, get off that bucket!" I said, "You ain't at home!" 'Cause out there them people are hostile—some of 'em. And he didn't like it.

But anyway, after that storm blew over we decided we had to hitchhike on into Tucumcari, New Mexico. So Mona went up the road a little ahead of me, and I stayed back, and I never did see him no more. I went on down into El Paso, and then on to the West Coast. And then I bumped into this Howard Carney from Chicago again. And Miss Jersey was out there, too. So the three of us decided we'd come on back to New York together. So we come back across on the Southern Pacific, and then we went up through Tennessee and Wheeling, West Virginia, and then we come into Newark, New Jersey. After we got back to New York I never did hear no more from

Howard Carney. I later heard that he had gone back to Seattle, Washington—that's where he was from—and died there in the street, drunk. Miss Jersey stayed around in New York and later turned into bein' a heroin addict. I did see Mona Brown in New York one day. I was livin' on Sixth Avenue, next block from Radio City Music Hall theater, and I happened to be lookin' out the window and saw him across the street. But that el was up there then, and it made a lotta noise. They were diggin' that subway down there at the time, but the el was still up, so he couldn't hear me when I yelled to him from up in the window. I run downstairs, but time I got down there he had done disappeared. We used to correspond, but he never did write no more after that. He was a campy queen.

Well, it was right before that farewell tour that I had met this guy named Henry Ethridge. He was a procurer. In them days you could always find some old faggots who was smart enough that if they'd see a good-lookin' boy, and he seemed pliable and willin' to go, and they trusted him, they'd say, "Gimme your phone number. Will you go out?" So they would procure for the rich, just like some of the madams in some of the whorehouses. There was one who catered to commercial artists, there was one who catered to writers, there was another one catered to just the general public, and there was dollar joints and call girls.

So one night on the Avenue there was this colored queen who had a set of keys in his hand, and he kep' shakin' them keys. I wondered at the time how he got into the neighborhood, 'cause you didn't usually see no blacks in that part of town at night. But he come up shakin' them keys and asked me if I wanted to go. I said, "Go where?" He said, "Down here to my house." He said, "I live right down the street." So he had this place on 56th Street, right down the street from where I was livin' with Leo Elmore. He had a white man pose like he was livin' and comin' in there, and this black guy was s'posed to be the butler, 'cause blacks wasn't s'posed to be livin' in that neighborhood then. But his name was Henry Ethridge. He was about 35 years old, and this place where he lived was a massage parlor—or really a whorehouse. Call-girl place. So he asked me where I lived, and I said, "I live right down here, a few doors down the street." And he said, "You wanna go out on dates?" I said, "Sure." He said, "Well I can use you." So I gave him the number of the phone right outside the door of my apartment, and he began to call me and send me out on dates. Leo Elmore and me was livin' at 66 West 56th Street in a room with runnin' water in it. The bath was down the hall, and there was a pay telephone right outside the door. So it was handy. 'Cause when I met Ethridge I come off the street and went on call.

Ethridge told me all about how he'd gone to school in upstate New York and was studyin' voice at Syracuse University, and how he'd worked in the drag shows on the line at night. Hustlin' the drag at night and went to college in the daytime! He loved to give concerts in New York. He would rent Town Hall for 500 dollars and give out all these tickets to the whores and pimps. There was days he'd make good money and days he wouldn't make good money. But he always had a buck.

Before I met Ethridge I'd mostly been around people in the park. I had no social contacts. All I knew was the goofers and the thieves and the whores and the junkies and everything. But when I met him a whole new world opened up for me, because he introduced me to all the madams and the people who had the call houses, and he introduced me to the nightlife scene in Harlem. And he'd send me out on dates for exhibitions, dates to have relations with broads and screw 'em, and all such as that. 'Cause most of these old men who go to these prostitute places, they can't do nothin'. They just wanna be *around* it. And they feel sorry for the prostitutes, so they wanna call in somebody who's gonna give 'em a good lay. So I had to learn to control, and not pop my rocks and spit every time with one of them prostitutes. 'Cause I saw how other kids who couldn't do that was deterioratin' and goin' down, man. They was beginnin' to dry up into a shell. So I thought, "Well, that ain't no good. I'll have to learn to control that thing." So I did, and I learned to fake ecstasy pretty good.

But Ethridge would send me here, he'd send me there, outta town or anywhere—Washington; Dover, Delaware; Pittsburgh; Buffalo; and up in Connecticut; in Westchester County. He knew all these people who wanted material—who wanted some boys. So it just opened up a complete new world for me. He'd send me to all these places on the train to meet these people who had a lotta money and big houses with servants. He'd say, "This is Mr. So-and-so, he lives in that town. You catch a train or catch a taxi and go to his house. He'll be expectin' you." It was just one thing after another like that—in office buildings, in basements and all kinda shit. A lot of 'em would tell you they were artists, and some of 'em had easels set up, makin' out like they was. They'd use that for an excuse to get you there and get you to take your clothes off.

All the artists and illustrators useta come to them whorehouses, man, to try to act out the scenes that they had to illustrate. They'd grab the whores by the hair of their head and throw 'em down, or come in wantin' to beat 'em and all that kinda shit. I didn't realize it at the time, but as I'm older now, I think they must've been livin' out them fantasies they was gonna put down in their illustrations or tryin' to get a certain amount of lust and sex to it.

All I'd have to do in them days was just lay back by the phone and wait for it to ring. And 'round 11 o'clock it'd start ringin', and they'd send you to this apartment house or that hotel, to Brooklyn, Queens, Uptown, Downtown, offices—everywhere. Ethridge had a lotta guys that wanted to suck your dick or wanted you to fuck 'em up the ass. Well, I couldn't do that, unless it was somebody that turned me on.

Which was dam', *dam'* rare. One out of a thousand, I would say. But when somebody wanted a terrific cocksucker, man, then Ethridge'd call me, 'cause I could do a blow job that wouldn't quit. I was what you call a "union girl." I could take it to the hair.

We had all these interesting dates and all these interesting places that we went. And sometime they'd take you out for dinner. So I found out I didn't need the street no more. But still I'd occasionally go cruisin' the Avenue. I'd generally walk through Fifth Avenue between 11 and 12 and make a score and pick up somebody who had been to the theatre. Sometime it would be men and sometime it would be women. Sometime it would be men who had their secretaries and couldn't give 'em a good time in bed, so they'd wanna pick up some nice young guy and take 'em and get 'em taken care of. It was just all kinda things, man—sadistic people, people who wanted to beat you, people who wanted to be punished and all that stuff. There was even one freak—a doctor from Chicago—who wanted to take a razor blade and split the skin here on the side of his stomach. I often wondered why he did that. I guess he had to have the nerve to cut himself in order to cut other people's skin. He didn't particularly care for me, because I didn't particularly care for all of that. I went with him a couple or three times, just to see what it was about, but it didn't give me any thrill at all.

These sex experiences that I had, I often used to wonder, "Why the fuck did I go on with this?" Of course there was the money there, but sometime without money. And it would seem like there was some spirit in me that was enjoyin' this pleasure through this person, and not me. I couldn't figure that out then. It's only in later years that I figured that that must've been the purpose there—it was a spirit enjoyin' the ecstasy through me through this person. Because I wouldn't get a kick out of it all, but yet I would go, and it was as if I couldn't *help* myself from goin'. I used to catch the subway, man, and go way out to the end of the line and walk back, cruisin' cops or anything else that I liked. I would say, "I'm gonna look for a beautiful freak tonight." And I would generally find one that was pretty good-lookin'.

But a lotta this stuff that was goin' on didn't turn me on. I liked my kicks private, and me and the person private, not with other people around. Now every once in a while, if it was one of these old men who wanted his prostitute taken care of and couldn't do it himself, and if it was a very beautiful whore, and if the guy had some attractions for me, well, I'd get on and have a ball. I could really come on like a fuckin' *gang*buster, man! So the guy would say to Ethridge, "Get him tomorrow." And here I'd come next day and, man, it'd be a different whore, and she might not be appealin' to me like the other one was. *Blank!* Well, that was farewell to that. They didn't want you no more. But I've always responded to what struck my viberations. If it didn't have no viberations, I couldn't respond.

Well, when it was one of these things when I wasn't turned on, I knew I had to come up with *some*thin', so I began to come up with these stories I'd tell and this line of bullshit that I'd talk. Or some freaky conversations which would turn people on. So that way I was more accepted, and they'd wanna keep me around longer. Some would call me just for that, and that's about the only thing I got a lotta repeats on. Some would call me to come over, and they'd say, "You make the place lively. You make it jump." So I would tell freaky stories like, *"Man, I was up in Harlem last night, man, and a goddam' big black nigger drugged me and grabbed me and knocked me in the head, took me in the alley and shoved it up my ass, and man, I thought he'd never get through!"* And man, that makes them bastards *cream,* y'understand.

There was this one whore named Chickie who was noted for tellin' freaky stories, too. She'd been a chorus girl at the Cotton Club in

Harlem, had a nice build, big tits. So if there was a john there and they couldn't get him to cream, they'd call me and her to come up with a story. She was known for it, and she'd recommend me to 'em. If she got a call and already had somethin' else lined up, she'd throw it to me. Chickie later developed consumption, T.B., went out to Colorado and cured it and came back.

Well, all this time I was on call for Ethridge I was livin' with Leo Elmore. He was a good hustler and was willin' to carry his share. So when we learned to get the big johns, then we moved outta this room where we'd been stayin' and moved into a little better place, an apartment. And we was hustlin' and goin' on calls, goin' to these after-hours spots. When the clubs closed downtown, that was when Harlem started to jump. That is, for a certain class of people—sporting people, who didn't have to get up in the mornin'. And all up there in Harlem it was a jumpin' town. Wasn't no thievin' goin' 'round. You could hear all kinda sounds—African, Caribbean, jazz.

I remember the first time I went up to Harlem was when Ethridge took us to the Theatrical Grill, where the black female impersonator Gloria Swanson held sway in all her regalia. And they had a hoot'n'tooty band there. They could really jam and get it on. And the shim-sham-shimmy was in vogue then. And Black Gloria Swanson would tie his prick and balls back behind his legs and come out and pick up dollar bills offa the tables. He'd learned how to maneuver a dollar bill through the crack of his legs.

We'd go up to Harlem two or three nights a week. Every Saturday night, and maybe on Tuesday, maybe on Thursday. Sometime it'd be every night. It depended on how much money you made. If you made good pennies, you'd go out and, *bang!* Have you enough to get back home and buy somethin' to eat in the mornin'. And the next day was another day, and the money would come rollin' in. I didn't hardly ever pay the bill at them places in Harlem, though. I was taken there by different people. We'd go to Small's Paradise, the Theatrical Grill and the Cotton Club, where Duke Ellington would be playin', or Cab Calloway. Noble Sissle, Lionel Hampton—I liked all of 'em that could play jazz and get it on, make you feel it. But we'd stay at them clubs in Harlem just about all night, until they closed, then we'd go out to a movie and wind up at one of those after-hour spots. It'd go on till all hours of the mornin'. Then we'd go down to Ethridge's bordello, and there we'd wine and dine some more till about one in the afternoon. Then we'd stagger back down to the subway and go get some sleep until evening, when we'd start back up all over again.

But it was Ethridge that introduced me to all this—to these madams and these whorehouses and these rich freaks, and to Harlem and all. He would've been Mayor of New York City if he hadn't've been black, 'cause he had so much moxie, man. He was very bold and brazen. There was never no sex between him and me, though. Well I might've sucked his dick maybe a few times, like if a freak wanted to see a white man suck a black man or somethin' like that. Ethridge had a way of gettin' a hard-on for most any-fuckin'-thing. Shit, man, it didn't turn me on. But I guess that's why he could build up like he did. He had a reputation for that. And he told me he fucked 'em all in the ass—that sooner or later they all had to have somebody penetrate their asshole. Married ones and all. They'd be come from the office buildin's downtown, stop off at his place, run back down and catch the subway or a car or whatever they was travelin' in, and be back on off to the wife.

I was with Ethridge for about a year, and then we fell out. 'Cause whenever he would get in a public place where you was with him, he would always bring up in the conversation that you was his girl and you was hustlin' for him and all such as that. So I didn't like that. It was annoyin' when he'd talk about you like that. And he wouldn't just mention it. He'd *harp* on it—"My two whores," and such as that.

And I give a party 'round that time, and I bought a lotta alcohol from the drug store and mixed up this shit they call bathtub gin, and I told this bitch to invite everybody worthwhile, but I didn't invite Henry Ethridge. Well, shit, I thought this bitch was gon' bring in some rich dudes, but all she brought in was a fuckin' buncha hustlers, man.

So for a while there I was in and outta Ethridge's graces. If he couldn't get nothin' else, he'd call me. If he could get somethin' else, he wouldn't call. He called others that lived with me, but he stopped callin' me.

All this time I had been livin' in New York I was studyin' human nature and lookin' at people and seein' different scenes—bulldykers, hustlers, whores, everything. So I was workin' on the psyche—developin' people, seein' people in clubs and gettin' their contacts. You know, as you get on up older, man, you learn who wants this and who wants that. Well, I learned to be sharp at lookin' at different kinds of people in the street and sizin' 'em up. So I was always on the lookout for young kids that'd come to town. They're out there to make a buck. They wanna survive, so they become flexible and pliable. So durin' the first few years after I fell out with Ethridge, bitches would come to town and certain people would tell 'em, "Go to the Countess. She's got connections." 'Cause I'd give my number to tricks and madams, and whenever they could work me in, why, naturally they got somethin' for it.

Y'see, I was gettin' older, and there was fewer and far less contacts. The phone didn't ring as often. I was gettin' *passé*. That's an expression bitches use. And elegant people.

So I began to do a little procurin' myself. I'd go to these after-hours places, and every time I'd see a nice-lookin' chick in there I'd say, "Gimme your phone number, honey, and I can give you some business." 'Cause I'd know she was hustlin'. That was the night life, and nothin' come into them places but hustlers and rich people. Or

I'd meet somebody, and I'd say, "I can get you some girls," or "I got some lovely boys."

I always kep' an eye to the future, so I knew what was comin', and I knew I wasn't gonna go to no nine-to-five routine. Although I did have a job in the summer of '37 as a usher at the Sam Harris Theater on 42nd Street. I got paid 11 dollars a week, and I had a room for five dollars, so that gave me six dollars to live on. But I got fired from that job, 'cause they caught me cruisin' the customers.

9. FROM PASSÉ QUEEN TO PASAQUOYAN

urin' one of my sojourns down here to Georgia—in 1935, right after Ethridge and me fell out—I got real sick, man, and I got weaker and weaker. I lost all motivation. And now that I'm older I realize that my spirit had done left my body and took a spiritual journey. It was gone. It just left me. I was in the bed for 10 or 12 days and wasn't eatin', and was just coughin' and heavin' up stuff. It seemed like I was cleansin' myself of my past. I gargled up all this phlegm, and it was like I was gettin' rid of all the evil and confusion that had welled up in me from years of not bein' myself. So one mornin' my sister come in, and she said, "Why, we was talkin' last night about goin' to send a coffin to get you this mornin' to bury you, 'cause we thought sure you'd be dead by now." They thought I had pneumonia, but we didn't have no money for no doctor. Or *I* had no money, and I didn't ask my mother for any.

But that night I come to, and I encountered this vision of this great

166

big character sittin' there like some kinda god, with arms big around as watermelons. He was bigger than a giant, man. He wasn't on a throne, but he was sittin' down. His hair went straight up, and his beard was parted in the middle like it was goin' straight up. And when I saw him I knew I had reached the end of my spiritual journey. And this great big man said to me, "If you can go back into the world and follow my spirit, then you can go, but if you can't follow my spirit, then this is the end of the road for you, and you can't go back." So I said, "Well, I'll do what you say." And then my spirit come back to me, and the next mornin' I began to get my strength. They began to feed me, and from there on I began to improve and get up. So I got up from there and broke the land and planted the crop, and took off for New York City.

I felt regenerated. Renewed. And it was then that I decided to be myself, regardless of the cost, regardless of the ostracism. Because, believe me, you get plenty of flak, man. But I listened to that inner voice, and I recovered, 'cause I had just had a new revelation.

That's when I really began to reach for the occult and for things that the average person don't know nothin' about. And I began to look back behind the scene, behind the façade, in all kinda religions. And then I realized that God had spoken to me, and that I was to follow his advice. So I said, "Just don't lead me to violence. Let it be something good."

You know, bein' what you wanna be in this life has a lot to do with luck, and bein' in the right place at the right time. But I wasn't ever there, it didn't look like, at the right time to be what I wanted to be. But I really didn't ever *know* what I wanted to be until I began to dabble in the arts and learned to depend on that inner voice. And then I began to be curious about all these religions. And I began to believe in myself.

I knew some artists at that time in New York, and I'd go up to their studios sometime and watch 'em work, and sometime they'd let me put a little paint on their canvases. And I began to draw. I couldn't afford canvases, 'cause the money wasn't rollin' in like it was when I was on call for Ethridge, so I'd pick up cardboard boxes from the street, and I would draw on 'em a little bit. I still got some of them drawin's from that time up in the loft here, if the rats and the bugs ain't eat 'em.

But it wasn't long after I come back to New York after bein' down here and gettin' sick that I read in an astrology book one day where it said, "On the 28th of May you'll start somethin' and you'll follow it the rest of your life." Well, I wondered, "What's gonna happen? Am I gonna meet somebody rich? Is somebody just gonna say, 'Well, now you can just paint, and I'll buy your paints and canvases and somethin' to paint with.'?"

So I wondered and wondered about it, and when that day come—the 28th of May, 19 and 35—I was settin' at the window in my apartment on 53rd Street, down the street from the Museum of Modern Art. It was between Fifth and Sixth Avenue. I lived up on the second floor. So anyway, I was settin' at the window there drawin' with a pencil on a piece of brown paper. And there had been a write-up in the magazine section of the *New York Times* about Haile Selassie, the Emperor of Ethiopia, and there was a picture of him in there. He appealed to me. I liked his type. So I started to draw a picture of him. And while I was drawin' him I noticed I could see this other figure from the brain inside. It was the image of a man's face with his hair long and swep' up, and somethin' told me that this is the natural image of man. That was a few years before I started growin' my hair and beard, but I remember seein' that face and thinkin' that at the time. And it was then that that inner voice spoke to me again and told me, "You're gonna be the start of somethin' new, and you'll call yourself *'Saint EOM,'* and you'll be a *Pasaquoyan*—the first one in the world."

That was before I knew any Spanish, but I found out later that *pasa* means 'pass' in Spanish. And *quoyan,* I found out, is a Oriental word that means 'bringin' the past and the future together.' So you can derive the benefits of the past by bringin' it into the future. And that's why I call myself a Pasaquoyan, and this place is called Pasaquan. Although I didn't know I was gonna build this place until I started doin' it, and that wasn't till about 20 years later. But that was that inner voice, which I've always let cue me which direction I would go ever since then.

Pasaquoyanism has to do with the Truth, and with nature, and the earth, and man's lost rituals. In the ancient days when man was created and put forth to walk on the face of this earth, he was given rituals by God. But man does not know those rituals any more. He's been robbed of 'em because of greed. He's so busy makin' a dollar that he's lost his rituals. Only man's labor is prized in this society. His love of soul and spirit and the earth will not be fully realized until he finds that he can communicate with his whole and natural body, including his hair and his beard.

It was when I started listenin' to that inner voice that I began to learn about the lost art of the hair and the beard. I had read in the Bible where it says, "Even the hairs on the head are numbered," and I said to myself, "Why're they numbered? There must be a purpose to it." So I began to observe different cultures, and to study the ancient hieroglyphics of the Egyptians and the Mayans, and I noticed that in the pictures they all seemed to have bound hair, pulled up on top of their heads, and sometime bound bodies. If you look at all these different dance costumes from different countries, you'll see that the body seems to be always tied or wrapped or bound in this colorful cloth. And if you look at the artwork of the Mayans you'll always see these people bein' pulled up by the hair of their heads, like they're bein' pulled up into the spirit world. And in them pictures they didn't seem like they was walkin'. They seemed like ethereal, floating people.

So I looked at the ancient art in the museums, and I got holt of this book of Mayan art called the *Kingsboro Edition,* where some Englishman copied all these inscriptions and hieroglyphics. And in that book it shows this god Quetzalcoatl sittin' with his legs crossed and his hair all bound up, and this thing stickin' out of it, and he's got his finger pointin' at his hair, like this. And when I saw that, I said to myself, "Well, that's a message there. It's tellin' you somethin' 'bout the hair." And then I started readin' these books by Sir James Churchward about the ancient days of Atlantis and Mu, and I saw that the people of those cultures all grew their hair up. And it had designs, and it sprouted out of their heads on each side, and there was a coil in the back. It was a complete entirety, all pulled together. And the hair up in these designs was just like lines of trees, 'cause if you keep pullin' 'em up, they'll stand up.

And you take other cultures, such as China and India and parts of Africa, where certain people had their hair growed up and pulled up. Then sometime in 1938 I saw a film about the Sikhs. The Sikhs was a tribe that was killed on sight by the Moslems in the beginning of the Moslem history in India. And they fought 'em off and survived, just like they're fightin' for survival today, and for a homeland of their own. And they kept their hair up. The Sikhs had a custom of cuttin' a child's hair like a bowl until he was 14 years old, and all that hair was pulled up and tied together. Then when he was 14 he started to turn the bottom part aloose, and the beard with it, and then he learned to braid that beard on a string and pull it up along the side of his face like I got mine here. So in this film I saw at one of the museums in New York, these Sikhs were doin' their morning rituals with their hair and their beard, and I thought, "Man, that's difficult! I think I'm gon' learn how to do that." And that's when I stopped cuttin' my hair and my beard and started lettin' it grow and pullin' it up and bindin' it.

So one day after my hair and beard had gotten kinda long I was cookin' rice, and I let it stay on the hot plate too long, and all this bubbly stuff was comin' up on top of it, and somethin' told me to take my brush and dip it in that hot goo and comb it into my hair and beard. Well, before I started doin' that it was stiff, but that rice syrup breaks it down. So I'd put that hot rice syrup on it and tie a piece of cloth on up around the top of my head, and put a turban around here to keep the hair all up. And I started doin' that every night. Then I would lay down, and all that would dry and begin to draw up, and I could feel it pullin' all down in my legs and all over my body. 'Cause the hair and beard controls the anatomy of the human skin and body. It's your antenna to the spirit world. It's your continuation of you in this universe—of your intelligence, your creativity, your common sense. It keeps you in contact with the planets. So, naturally, cuttin' and shavin' and twangin' on yo'self is against all those things, because there's a whole design that goes all in there with that. It's a mystery that man must fully know and understand before he can really call himself a man. And I useta take a needle with gold thread and do a box stitch all the way up the side of my face through my beard and put jewels in it.

You see, all these hairs here control a set pattern. I'd braid my hair into braids and pick that hair up in a half diamond, then leave a diamond in there, then braid that together. Well, this controls an entirety within this design and this pattern. This controls one here, this controls one over here, and this back here is a thing that comes in here like that, that's got them diamond things and mountaintop things goin' up into it, and it's like a pair of jaws or somethin' that

171

close there. There's great power in there, and great longevity of life by takin' care of these things. It's a high class art, but it's a hard thing to learn, man. It's very *difícil, señor*. And man is gonna go on down, down, down, until somebody can see the light and start to pull all this hair up and braid it and learn the art and the care of it and everything. If man could only learn it, it would keep his body from saggin' and growin' old. It would hold up the muscles of the hair, and all such as that. And I think man is easier to control with his hair and beard cut, and that's one of the ways this society uses to control man. The image that they got set for us is *all* planned, man. You see all these neurotic people runnin' around here with their hair and beards cut and disfigured. Some of the kids grow their hair long now, but they need to grow it *up*. Man's perspective's been dulled.

So these are the things that I went back and researched and looked into—into the past histories of cultures that's above the water and cultures that're under the water. And I come up with the conclusion that them people was on the right path. This path that we are on is the path of destruction. It's got to come together where people can be human beings, and be themselves, and not be concerned about what others think, but not do harm to others. With all the greed and the war and the militarism and all of that, people have got to sit down and say, "Somethin' has got to give. And it's not gonna be what we've had in the past. It's got to be somethin' different." And that difference is learnin' the art of the hair, and braiding of it, and controlling it to grow upward instead of downward. That's the secret that man has got to learn about his natural self and his health. But alas, I'm afraid it'll be lost, because I'm the only one that's dug into it this far.

When I began to find out about all these things I brought a whole new culture out there, man, onto the street, right in the heart of New York City. And it was ignored altogether. Occasionally I'd take a turn out in the streets, but it was useless to go out there tryin' to hustle anymore, 'cause wasn't nobody gon' pick you up with hair and a beard. So I just quit walkin' out there, although I'd walk down the Avenue just for exercise. Anyway, I was gettin' old, and people didn't want me anymore. They want youth.

After I stopped cuttin' my hair and my beard and started learnin' the art of takin' care of it and growin' it up, everybody said I was crazy, and they ignored me—even the prostitutes and the faggots. They wouldn't even stop and talk to me, man. I was really ostracized. But I was determined. It seemed like the whole world was turned down on me at that time, but I stuck it out and got through by the skin of my teeth. I said, "I'm not gon' cut my hair no more." And when I set my mind to somethin', I don't change. But after I turned my hair and my beard out, when all the whores and everybody that knew me would see me comin', they'd cross the street or run get in a taxi. They thought I had flipped my wig or somethin'.

After I couldn't hustle no more with the beard and the hair, I started playin' poker. I was good at it, and I'd generally come out the winner. I was goin' around different places gamblin', so I figured I'd just set up somethin' myself. I was livin' on 52nd Street at the time, upstairs over the Famous Door nightclub. That's where Martha Raye got her start, and Count Basie useta play there all the time when I was livin' upstairs. And from '38 to '42 I run poker games in my apartment on the weekends for the pimps and the whores and street hustlers, goofers, shake men and con men who was willin' to come and lose their money. I'd cut the pot and set on the side, and whenever I got sort of a hunch I went in, but if I didn't I'd stay out. And that's hard to do when you're playin' poker. But I would take speed then to gamble, and the rest of 'em were drinkin' alcohol. I'd sell beer and I'd make a big pot of chili and maybe some fried chicken, and I'd be gettin' up to serve everybody, but I kep' up with my tally on the pot. There was a few of us would smoke weed and get high—maybe four of us. The rest of 'em wanted whiskey. And durin' those days I useta get a little pot, and people would come buy it—not from me, but I'd get the money for the guy. First it started, the pusher would leave pot there for people, and I would collect the money for it. And then I thought, "Well, shit, fuck this! Why give him the money when I'm sellin' it?" So I started buyin' it by the ounce and rollin' joints and sellin' 'em six for a dollar. Small joints. And I would always keep 20 dollars to get another ounce after I sold what I was sellin'.

So downstairs every night Count Basie was swingin' at the Famous Door—"The One O'Clock Jump." The fuckin' buildin' would just rock with it, man. You could hear it all the way up on the top floor where I lived. And on the weekends was the poker games, and durin' the week I'd be flyin' to the Library at 42nd Street, the Museum of Natural History, the Metropolitan Museum. They have a lot at the Metropolitan Museum that they don't show to the general public. You have to put in a written request. They had a full story of things down in the basement. Ancient history and the primitive peoples— that was always what interested me. And I was studyin' the art of the hair and the beard.

Occasionally I'd run into somebody I knew from my hustlin' days, and they'd say, "What's wrong with you? You're not like you useta be." And I'd say, "Well, I don't wanna be like I useta be."

It was a very precarious thing, man.

10. LEXINGTON

hen the War come along the government started reachin' out for people for the Army. And I'd see a lotta people who was goin' down to be examined, and the Army wouldn't take 'em. So they'd come back, and I'd say, "What goes on down there?" And they hipped me to what went on: There was a certain sergeant down there, and if you mentioned to him that you were homosexual, and acted real bitchy, then that was the end of the line. And when you got to this sergeant, if you didn't turn back there, then there wasn't no turnin' back. So I was prepared for it, man. I went in there with my hair and beard and said, "Hey, I don't wanna fight no war!" Man, the yellow paper. That showed they didn't want you—that you were undesirable. So I didn't have to go.

Well, it was while the War was on, in 1942, that I got busted. I was at rope's end at the time, man. I was still livin' on 52nd Street over the Famous Door, but I was behind in my rent, and it was gettin'

175

hard to make a livin' with a beard and long hair. So one night these cops knocked on the door, and I let 'em in. They didn't have no search warrant or nothin', but I let 'em in anyway. They said I was sellin' marijuana. They didn't have no sale on me, so I said, "Sale where?" And they said, "That silver dollar." Well, this pot pusher I knew named Gregory had done got busted, and his old lady had give me a silver dollar. So she musta thought I turned him in or somethin'. 'Cause when them cops said that, then I knew that bitch had done put the finger on me. The cops'll always let you know if somebody squeals on you. I've never seen it fail. So they said, "If you don't tell us where it is we gon' tear this place apart." Well, they found six joints in the drawer, so I got busted. And it was either go to jail or turn to bein' a stoolpigeon. I wouldn't've had to go to jail if I'd snitched on others. They said, "Tell us the name of three more, and you can go." And they was tryin' to take me to some restaurant to eat or somethin', but I said, "Where you gon' take me? Take me there." I said, "I have nothin' to say to you, I have nothin' to tell you. In fact, I don't even *like* you!" And I said, "If you're gon' kill me, kill me. If you're gon' take me to jail, take me there." So they took me there. Opened this big steel door, man, and "SLAM!" Into the cell with the junkies—Chinese heroin addicts they'd rounded up that night, and American junkies, too. The Chinese was sittin' there just as calm as hell, man, just takin' in the misery. And the Americans were just *groanin'* and *dyin'*, and "*Ohhh,* my God!" And I saw just how strong the Chinese race is. It was all just amazin' to me. I hadn't been through it before. So I thought, "Shit, this is a new experience!"

Well, durin' all these years I had talked to people who had been to the federal narcotics prison hospital in Lexington, Kentucky—that's the prison they had there for the heroin addicts and the marijuana people, too. And they told me the most fascinatin' stories 'bout how the local farmers there had 50-acre fields of pot growin' just a mile or a mile and a half from the prison fence. Cultivated marijuana—hemp—for makin' ropes. And I thought to myself, "Jesus, that'd be all right!"

So I had to stay in jail for six weeks waitin' for a trial. And I met a guy in the jail who had been to Lexington, and he was tellin' me about it. He said, "Man, if you have to go there, then volunteer to work on the prison farm. Don't go into the industries inside the prison." He said, "Man, when I was there I was on the dairy, and I'd jump the fence and make a run every two or three weeks and get a sackful." Well, when I heard that I thought it was the most *thrillin'* thing, man! So I really wanted to go to Lexington. When I finally went to court the judge offered me a chance to talk, and I said, "I have nothing to say. What you're gonna do, do." And they said, "Will you sign here that you're guilty?" And I said, "Yes, I'll sign 'guilty.'" So the judge sentenced me to a year and a day in Lexington. Right before I got busted I had done won 20 dollars in a poker game, and this fuckin' lawyer come down while I was in jail and says, "I'll help you." Well, he didn't open his dam' mouth! I give him my last 20 dollars, and when I got to Lexington I had nothin'.

Well, when I got there I wasn't no more than inside the gate when here comes this superintendent of the prison tellin' me that I had to cut my hair. And I told him, I says, "I'm not cuttin' my hair." I says, "I come here for my *health!* I didn't come here to impair my health." I told 'em I was a Sikh, and I said, "My hair is my religion. I come here with it, and I'm gon' leave here with it." And I left with it. They didn't cut my hair. They wanted to. But while I was in there I useta take these wrappin's that they wrap around your legs, and I'd wrap 'em around my head, and I'd put some kinda wool cap over it where they couldn't see it. But somebody told 'em that I was doin' it, so one day they frisked me at the gate, and they took that wrappin' away from me. But I useta hold my hair up with that—wrap it around my head very heavy. And I got holt of a couple of bed sheets, and I sewed 'em together and made a turban and dyed it purple, and was wearin' that, but they took it away from me after 'bout a week.

But when I first got to Lexington they put us in quarantine for two weeks—that's in a ward grouped together—to observe you and get your reaction and see how you're gonna adjust and acclimate to the thing. And durin' that time you had to work on the mop squad, and you was under surveillance. I hated the mop squad.

But there was civilians and prisoners in there, 'cause civilians could just come in and register and take a cure there. They had whirlpool baths and saunas and everything, man. I met a doctor from Atlanta who was in there. He was a civilian who had come there for a cure. He was a beautiful bastard, too, but I never could get him. He wasn't there too long. They could sign themselves in and sign themselves out. And the rest were all prisoners. I reckon there was about seven or eight hundred of us.

Well, after the two weeks in quarantine was up, then you went before the board, and they'd ask you where you wanna go or what you wanna do. You could be in the sewin' factory where they made suits of clothes, or you could be in the carpentry shop, or you could be in an office, or you could be on the farm. Well, I had been hipped about the farm—that was where you could get over the fence and score your pot. So when it come to my turn I didn't even wait for them to ask me. I said, "I wanna go to the farm." And I said, "I come from a farm, and I know how to work on one." So they assigned me to the farm.

Well, for the first 30 days out on the farm you was under guard. You couldn't get away. But after 30 days you made trusty. So the first day I went out on detail they put me on a big 50-acre patch of tomatoes. 'Cause we grew all the food for the prison. And while I was hoein' I spied a big stalk of pot growin' back up in the weeds where the truck didn't pass too close to it.

I was told that before I got there pot growed all up in the yards of the prison. The people who run the place didn't even know what it was. And then they finally got wise to what it was. That's the way I heard it. And after that them doctors' wives would ride around on horses and pull up the pot plants when they come up in the spring. The birds shit the seeds out, and quite a few would come up. But this one I spotted out there in the field was one they'd done missed.

Well, by this time I'd started to learn more or less who was to be trusted, and who it was good to know in the prison. The Mudbugs outta New Orleans had the most important places. That's what they called the guys from New Orleans, was Mudbugs. They had the decent places, and had a little say-so in the prison, I guess 'cause there was so dam' many of 'em in there. Anyway, they could stash.

So I hoed out my row there in the tomato patch. I knew how to hoe, so I hoed ahead and finished, and the others were just startin', really. So I set there a little bit, and then the guy come by in the truck—the guy who hauled the hands out to the tomato field. He was a Mudbug. So I sneak into the truck, and he drives me over there to where this pot was growin', and I run up this ditch and snatch this plant out, and we bring it out. The Mudbugs was what you call the smugglers in the prison, who'd move somethin' from one place to another, so I give it to them, and I got about three or four joints from it.

I got friendly with the head Mudbug on the farm, who fed the horses. And he was in charge of these big bales of hay, stacked 10 or 12 feet high, for the horses, and that's where they'd hide the pot—under them bales of hay. So I found some more pot plants around in different places out on the farm. Them doctors' wives weren't as observant as I was. So I'd turn it over to the Mudbug, and then I'd get a few joints outta that, and the others would get high. And the Mudbug brought me cigarettes. I hadn't ever smoked cigarettes, but he said, "Well, I can't give you nothin' else. You done brought all this pot. We buy in cigarettes and pay in cigarettes." So he gave me a few cartons. Well, I'd smoke 'em and give 'em away. But I never did inhale tobacco. First I smoked Bull Durham, till later on, after I got over the fence and scored the pot from the farmers' fields. Then I could get anything I wanted.

After that first 30 days was up and I'd done made trusty and wasn't under guard no more, I was ready to go over that fence and score some of that cultivated marijuana from them hemp farms, man. And by the second mornin' after I made trusty I had done learned all the information. They had a regular map, the prisoners did, that they kep' out on the farm. And it showed just where to go—to this fence, up this ditch, 'cross over yonder to that other fence, and you're there. So they showed me their map, and the next mornin', man, I get up real early, and I get out there and I head over that fence with a croker sack. And I go there in this field and I break down these plants. They're still green then, 'cause it was just early in the summer. But I get a croker sack full, I come back, I take it to the tomato field that afternoon with the guy that's haulin' the horseshit—he was a Mudbug— and we take it out there where we'd done hoed the tomatoes, and we lay it down to let it dry. And then a couple of days later we get it, and me and this Mudbug that takes care of the horses, we go down in the center of them stacks of hay till we get down to the floor, and we put the pot in there. But we keep maybe a pound out, and we hide it under the horse trough, or I'd cover it up with feed or something like that. They'd come out to search it every once in a while, but they'd only go down about five layers into the hay, and then they'd get tired. They wouldn't go all the way down to the bottom, so they never did find it. But through the pot man you was able to get anything, 'cause he'd trade pot for different things. So I'd send a Bull Durham sack of pot to the kitchen by way of him and say, "I want some meat, I want some cakes, I want some this, I want some that."

But anyway, that that I got when it was green lasted us, then, till October. And that's when them hemp farmers were thrashin', and it's layin' there dried in big piles—five feet high and 10 foot long, nothin' but thrashed out there. So I went back then and got another sackful. I made five trips over and back while I was there. I kept the Mudbugs happy and myself happy. They kept me supplied till the day I left. So I'd smoke up in the daytime outside while I'd be drivin' a wagonload of horseshit pulled by two horses to scatter it in the field every day.

That prison was a wild place, man. A buncha doctors had this whole prison to watch after and take care of, and they was livin' like royal kings in these manor houses around on the far side of the reservation, livin' off the fat of the land, man, in luxury and style, with fine horses to ride and all these prisoners workin' in their houses like servants. Some of the prisoners was fuckin' their wives and all that shit, man, and some of 'em was even fuckin' the doctors! Amazing!

The head Mudbug at the prison, the one that fed the horses, was a guy named Carl somebody. I done forgot his last name. But he had a great big beautiful dick. And the first night I was there I went down to his cell and did a job on him. So I immediately started runnin' from cell block to cell block. But there was this Puerto Rican stoolpigeon queen in there, and she told on me. So this old Doctor Preston called me in and said, "We have just the nice place for you. It's called 'isolation.' " He said, "You don't lock up until nine o'clock at night, and you're open at six in the mornin'." And I said, "Well, that suits me fine, because I'm on the farm, and all I do after I come in is eat and go to bed and sleep. So it doesn't matter whether the door's open or not. 'Cause I'm gonna be asleep, probably, when they do slam it at nine o'clock." And I thought to myself, "Well, it'll remind you what a prison is, to be locked up every night. So it'll make you work to keep the fuck outta there." So I went on up to isolation, and it was all bitches up there. They isolated the gay population—those that were promiscuous, that is. Those that had lovers, that just had *one,* was allowed to stay in population. But if you went with more than one you couldn't stay in population.

I useta come up in the elevator, then I'd go to the window and look out through the bars, and I'd think, "Well, you only got six more months." Or "four more months," or whatever. "Then you'll be outta this place. Just don't fuck up while you're here." Of course I took a chance goin' over the fence for that pot. But a couple of 'em went over and got caught, and they didn't do nothin' to 'em. They didn't extend their time any longer.

Isolation suited me just fine, though. At six o'clock the door was open, and I'd get up and eat breakfast, and I was gone to the farm. At 12 o'clock I'd come back in the gate, and you could eat and go on to your cell. There was an old auntie nigra who also lived up in isolation, and she worked in the kitchen. Well, she always was the courier. She'd bring pork chops and steaks and all that shit up from the kitchen, man, and we'd cook 'em on this electric plate we had up there.

There was this big, colored mulatto faggot named Sweet Pea that was in isolation, too. He was there doin' two years for pushin' heroin in Washington, D.C. She was about six foot two, half white, half black. On junk. Liked young boys. She had palsy, and her hands shook like this. She was nice to me, though, and we got along all right. She got some brown paper for me in the kitchen or somewhere, and stole me some watercolors outta some box he saw. So I used those to draw me some paintin's, and I hung 'em all over the walls in my cell. They were just landscapes with trees and a long perspective, with a road goin' off in the distance toward the horizon. And then I drew a couple of the heads with the hair goin' up. I left 'em there when I left in '43. I didn't bring 'em out.

But Sweet Pea was one of the ones that cleaned out the cells where they put 'em in solitary when they'd fuck up, and put 'em on bread and water. And she stashed pot for me. She'd keep it in the mattresses up there in them cells she cleaned. And sometime she'd make up my bed for me, 'cause I didn't make it up every mornin'. They'd make all the rest of 'em make up their beds, but the guard would say, "He works. He ain't got time to make up no bed. He don't feel like makin' up no bed."

But to me that cell was just a place to sleep and eat. My life was out on the farm. I had done made my contacts, so all I had to do was tell the Mudbug I wanted so-and-so to have a bag of butter, 'cause a couple of 'em wanted to bake cakes, or I'd tell him we wanted some steaks from the slaughterhouse, or anything where there was somethin' you could get aholt of.

Pot was always available at the prison. Speed was there all the time. There was a guy that lived in isolation that sold the speed, and gambled, too. Every Sunday he went out and didn't come back till way in the evenin'. He wouldn't even come home to eat. He'd been gamblin' and sellin' speed. There wasn't no cocaine in the prison. Junk got in occasionally. There was a drummer there who had been in Duke Ellington's band, and another one who had been with Fletcher Henderson, but they had done sunk too low to play in them bands no more. They was two of the ones who was fuckin' with junk there in the prison, when they could get it. One time a guy brought down a pound of opium and throwed it over the fence. I went and got that and brought it to the guy it was intended for. It was like a great big hunk of coal. He throwed it over in a burlap bag, and I knew where he was gon' throw it. It was quite a run to go there and get it, too, 'cause you had to cover about three miles there in about 40 minutes, was all the time you had to get it. You had to run your fuckin' ass off, man. Some of the guards brought in pot, and the prisoners were pushin' it for 'em, and they were dividin' the money.

One time I brought some pot in, and I went in Sweet Pea's cell, and I laid it up on the bunk. And here come the guard. He got curious or somethin', and he come down there to look. Well, Sweet Pea laid a newspaper over it. So the guard didn't lift up the newspaper or nothin'. But one day he said to me, "I know you're bringin' stuff in here, but you don't give me no trouble, and you mind your own business." So he laid offa me. He didn't bother me.

Occasionally they'd strip you naked at the gate and search you. One time they searched me I had a chain around my neck, and I had the pot tied to this chain, and it was hangin' down my back. Well, somehow or another I maneuvered for him to search me, and I kept turnin' my back, and he never did see that pot that was hangin' down my back. It was in a Bull Durham bag I had tied onto this chain.

But every morning I'd get breakfast and go to the farm. And every day before I'd go back in I'd always roll a big joint and hide it in the grass. And if it was rainin' I put it in a Prince Albert can, and if it didn't look like it was gonna rain I'd just hide it in the grass. Well, by the time I'd get a hundred feet from the gate every mornin' I would pick up this joint and light up, man. And there was a big room out on the farm there where we smoked pot every morning. There wasn't nothin' in there. It was just an empty room. And I did big Buddhas and murals on the walls. They was gon' spoil 'em out once, but they changed their mind. I wonder if they're still there. That was the first time I'd ever handled a big space. I could've got into the craftsmen's room at the prison, but I had heard that you get in these places and you're a good craftsman and can learn and show people, they keep you from gettin' out. They prolong your release and all that shit. So I thought, "Well, I don't wanna fuck with that. 'Cause I wanna get outta here quick as I can."

I got along with the other prisoners wonderful. I didn't have no trouble. Everybody liked me. I didn't come in contact with many of 'em after I got on the farm and got put in isolation, though. All I'd do was come in the gate, go through the prison up to the main lobby and catch the elevator, go up to the sixth floor to my cell. And otherwise I didn't come in contact with 'em unless I went down to watch the ballgame, which they played once in a while. But that didn't interest me. Out there on the farm I had who I wanted to pick and who I wanted to choose. And I was always cruisin', lookin' for things.

This big Texan was my first lover out on the farm. He had done come in with this buncha prisoners they brought in from Fort Leavenworth, and they put him out on the farm drivin' the horseshit wagon. And one day right after he got there me and him was in the toilet, and he was takin' a leak, and he started shakin' it. He said, "You like this?" I said, "Yeah, it's all right!" And I said, "What about gettin' some of it." And he said, "Well, when we go out on the horse wagon, we'll get to town." So I done him that morning, and he told me before we went to lunch, he said, "I want it again." And I said, "We'll go down in the bullpen." They had an old bull down there that was a stud, so I went down there and locked him up in a pen, and I was standin' in this place waitin' for him, and here he is comin' down this corral into this farm thing where them bulls stayed, and man, time he hit there his hard was on and shinin' in his hand. He was rarin' to go. And man, it was really wonderful. I useta catch him and he'd have to go two or three times. He couldn't help it. He'd been in prison for so many years, and he hadn't had no lovers or nobody. He said he'd done been in for 15 years. But all of a sudden they just released him. And when he left he said, "Man, I really hate to leave you." He said, "When you get outta here you come to Fort Worth." But I didn't go to Fort Worth.

I was lucky, though. I always picked a guy that was only gonna have a couple of weeks or another three weeks left there to do, and that way it was continuous. I didn't get hung up on one thing. And that made things move fast. You was with this one, and he was gone, then you were onto another one, then he was gone, and so forth and so on. So from that Texan I went on to a couple of Puerto Ricans, then another guy, and they was gone. I liked the Puerto Ricans. They was small and they was cute—some of 'em was. Some of 'em looked like monkeys.

On Sunday we'd go out to this pasture where you was allowed to go out and walk around, and there was a lotta sycamore trees out there. So I'd meet my friends and go up in the trees and do 'em up there, 'cause these fuckin' guards was ridin' around checkin', on horses. And we'd be up in the trees. They would sit on a forked limb and I would give 'em head jobs. They was willin' to take the chance, and I was, too. I had some beauties up there in them sycamore trees, man.

They had a movie house in the prison where every Saturday they showed movies. I saw a couple of Greta Garbo movies there. The others I don't remember. But durin' the movies was always a cruisin' time. The lights was down, and you could go back in the seats and cop somebody's joint if you wanted.

Mine was always the older men, older than 45, or around that age. I never went for youth. Youth never appealed to me. 'Cause I knew how people corrupted my youth, which I was willin' for 'em to do. But I figured, "Well, shit, I don't wanna be bothered with breakin' nobody in."

I even had a guard, man! He just come over that one day, and he kep' lookin' at me, and I knew he wanted to go with me. So I hung back from lunch and didn't go to lunch, and we went up in the hayloft and had a ball. But he never did come back no more. He was just there for that day. And Old Man Brooks, who was my boss, he wanted to go one time, 'cause he said, "Come on, Whiskers . . ."—he called me "Whiskers." He said, "We gonna go back way over yonder and check on that corn." There wasn't no checkin' to do. He thought I was gon' make a break at him, but he didn't appeal to me, so I just rode over there with him. He got disappointed. That's what he had in mind. He was just an old local farmer that had a job in there.

I didn't fool with just anybody. I picked kinda stable people. There was a lotta speed in that prison, and a lotta speed freaks. And you had to watch out for them, because they couldn't ever come or get a hard-on. A couple of 'em I attempted that worked up in the firehouse, and I said, "Man, you're too high on speed to get this thing up." So I didn't bother with that no more.

Not far away was a women's prison called Arlington. And once in a while them women would bust out, and some guys from the prison would bust out, and they'd meet down there in that pasture. That happened a couple of times, but they stopped that—put a closer watch on 'em. And not far away, close enough where you could see it, was a reform school for boys. Ooooh, man, they useta beat the *shit* outta them guys. You could see 'em beatin' 'em when we'd be workin' over on that side of the reservation. A couple of 'em escaped one time, and they caught 'em. Oh, they just beat the hell out of 'em. It was really disgraceful. They had all these fuckin' rednecks in there as guards. Local people. Ignorant.

There was this old horse at the prison called Minnie. She was an old bitch. She had been in the World War and all. But she was pretty. And you could go and pat her on the ass, man, she'd back out and spread her legs, ready to get it. See, these guards would fuck her. I'd go by and pat her on the ass, but I wouldn't fuck her. So she hated me. When I'd go by and pat her on the ass, she'd stomp the floor like that, mad as hell. But she was one of the horses that I drove haulin' manure from the dairy out to put on the crops. I took over that job when that lover from Texas got out. And sometime I worked out in the field.

One time some people was out there shootin' a film of us workin' in the field with the corn. But they eliminated me out of it. They cut me out. They didn't leave me in atall. That's when I was wearin' the purple turban.

And then one time the prisoners was gon' put on a show, and I was gon' do a dance in it. I was gon' do one of my twistin' and shakin' numbers, with a drum. I had a good drum, and there were some pretty good musicians in there, too. So we had a rehearsal, and right after I finished rehearsin' my number the head man called me to his office and said, "You can't dance in that show. I can't let you go on that stage." Said, "You might cause a riot." But it was all right with me. I said, "Well, I can't dance, then." I said, "It ain't gon' kill me." That was the only time I got to see the head guy. What the fuck was his name?

Sweet Pea, that bitch who lived up in isolation with me, worked over in the psychiatrist's office, where he was testin' all kinda shots they'd give you where you'd never lie. Truth serum. And the prison record room was over there, too. So Sweet Pea looked up my record in the files, and in the file it said I come from a weird family, and there was three brothers, and they all liked to dress up in women's clothes. Well, that wasn't true. I was the only one that dressed in women's clothes. This was old Doctor Preston who had written this about me. He was the same one who sent me to the isolation ward.

I spent nine months and 18 days at Lexington. My sentence was a year and a day, but you could get so much time off for good behavior— 'bout three months—and I didn't fuck up. I didn't get in fights and all such shit as that. I minded my own business, and I didn't try to give the authorities a hard way to go. If they said, "Well, you got to do this," I did it.

So on Saint Patrick's Day, the 17th of March, 19 and 43, I made my exit. There was one guy—the superintendent on the farm, Old Man Brooks—come to say goodbye. He was the only one. I smoked two joints before I went down to go through the rigamarole, where they search you, frisk you down, take off your shoes.

I went out high.

11. THE HOWDY CLUB

All durin' these years that I had been livin' in New York there were these two queens, Mel Stone and Bay Baker, who was runnin' these speakeasy joints, where they sold liquor durin' Prohibition. And they was always gettin' raided. Well, after Prohibition was over, they got in with some racketeers and opened up the Howdy Club, down in the Village south of Washington Square, on West Fourth Street. The Howdy Club was an old landmark. It was known all over the world, and it run for years and years. I had never thought about tryin' to get a job there until I come outta the clink in 1943. I had three months probation to report, and I was supposed to try to find a job. The War was still on, and the government was reachin' for everybody to put you in shipyards and all that shit. But I didn't wanna be bothered with that.

When I come back to New York in 1943 I cut my hair, 'cause I knew I'd have to do it to get a job. But I didn't have nothin' to wear

but that old prison suit. So this pimp I knew named Jack Daniels—
"*Miss* Daniels," he was called by the bitches—he loaned me a suit of
clothes. He always had a couple of whores fussin' around and takin'
care of him. And he knew this Bay Baker at the Howdy Club very
well. In fact, he got boys for him. And Bay Baker knew me, but I
wasn't his type. Bay Baker liked these rough character types—these
types that are real mean and evil. They stand around and wanna beat
up faggots and all, but they're just as crazy as the faggots are. That's
the type she liked. She didn't like me, 'cause I screamed and hollered
and yelled and carried on, put on makeup, paint, mascara and all that
kinda shit. But I always had a way of carryin' myself with a dignity,
regardless. Whether it was swish or whatever, you know, there was a
certain amount of class to it. It wasn't like no country hick come to
town. But anyway, Miss Daniels told Bay, "The Countess needs help."
He said, "He can't get no job, and you need people here." And said,
"Give him a job." So he come and told me, he said, "Go on down to
the Howdy Club. Bay Baker'll give you a job up in the balcony there."
So I went down there and I took a job as a cocktail waiter. I wasn't
supposed to be workin' in no place that served alcohol, so I told my
probation officer I had a job paintin' apartments.

The Howdy Club was famous for gays and lezzes. All of 'em that
worked there had been street hustlers, so they was very connivin'. But
they drew crowds. Bitches always packed the house. All the other
clubs might be starvin' to death, but the drag places, man, were packed
every night. Every night was Saturday night. Well, right away I began
to make money. I made good money there, for that time. I didn't
have no clothes after I come back from Lexington, so I had all kinda
suits and things to buy. So I bought me this great wardrobe, and I
thought maybe I might go out to Hollywood, but I didn't do it.

One reason I made such good money at that Howdy Club is that
there was always so many people in there that you could do things

without nobody seein' you. Like when I'd go to the bar to get a round of drinks I'd get to talkin' with the bartender and distract his attention while I was pourin' the drinks, and I'd let the booze run over the top of the glasses and into the tray. Then after I gave them drinks to the people who had ordered 'em I'd get their empty glasses and fill 'em up with the booze that had done spilt over into the tray, and I'd sell them drinks and pocket the money. And then sometime I'd even bring my own bottle into the club and sell drinks from that. I was always careful how I did it, though, and didn't nobody ever notice.

They would put on stage shows, song and dance numbers and so forth, at the Howdy Club, and all kinda performers would do their acts there. Eddie Gerden would perform there, and this Italian lezzie named Nikki. I can't remember her last name, but she would put on a sombrero and a Spanish suit of clothes, kinda like dancers wore, and she'd sing a Spanish song. She wasn't no sensational singer, but she was kin to the Italians that run the place—I think they was Mafia— and that's why she stayed in there. She was cute, too, and she was an attractor. She drawed the lezzies to the place. I was even in the show for a while, as a dancer in the chorus. There was a new show went in, and I thought, "Oh, I'm here, I should be in the show." And they thought I should be in there, too. I had been workin' there a few months by that time. The way they did it was Mel Stone would do one month's show, and then Bay Baker would put on the next show. So I was gonna do this dance to this Duke Ellington song, "Caravan." Well, I think I lasted 10 days, and I caught a awful cold runnin' down in that basement, man, changin' my clothes, and I'd be all hot and sweaty and have to run back up there and wait on them tables. And I thought, "Shit, this is interferin' with *my* welfare, here." So I just dropped out. They didn't ever say nothin' and I didn't ever say nothin'. They didn't pay you no more salary anyway. But it was a chance where you could've broke in a act if you'd been interested enough. But I realized that I was done on in years, and I had these tattoos on my body, so it was too late for me.

They had palm-readers and fortune-tellers downstairs at the Howdy Club, and there was one of 'em who was known as Prince Gene. I don't know what his real name was, but they called him Prince Gene. He was from Baltimore. Well, he wasn't makin' too much readin' palms, and he found out that I was makin' good money workin' up there in the balcony. So he come up there, and I said to myself that they sent him up there to watch me and dig me out for the bosses. So I set him down and I talked to him. I said, "Listen, you know this world is dog-eat-dog." And I said, "You tellin' anything you see or know about me ain't gonna do you no dam' good. These folks are racketeers here." I said, "And they're not gonna reward you. They'll do you in just as quick as they would anybody else." 'Cause there was gangsters in there all the time. The head knocker at the club was a guy named Stevie, and he later got found dead in the back end of some car trunk. They'd have shootin's in the club, and they'd just mop up the blood and go on with the show. So I told Prince Gene, I said, "You better come on my side. You come up to the balcony and work with me, and I'll see that you're rewarded." So I'd work, and I'd give him so much of what I made.

I worked at the Howdy Club for about two years, until May of 1945. They lost their license, so that was the end of that. So I hung around in New York there for three or four days, and I took my wits together. I had a few thousand dollars saved up. So I thought, "Well, I'll go back home." So I bought a round-trip ticket and caught the train and come home for the summer. I helped my mother on the farm—plowed the corn and hoed the cotton. That was in about May I came. So I stayed in May, June, July. And 'long about the first of

August, after the crop was laid by, I thought, "Well, I'll go back to New York. I can't take this. This is too much." So I went and presented my return-trip ticket and caught the train back to New York.

I hadn't cut my hair yet since right after I'd got outta the prison at Lexington, but when I got back to New York I cut my hair and my beard, 'cause I knew I had to look for a job. And in the meantime the Howdy Club had done opened up again in another spot—across town on Eighth Street. So I went down one night, and the guy that worked up in the balcony wanted to take the night off. He said, "You take my place tonight." So I took his place and made pretty good. Then the next night somebody else wanted to be off, and I took their place. Then the next night I went in, and they said no, no more for me. The guy there that owned it didn't like me. He didn't like my looks. I looked too sharp for him.

Well, when that happened I thought, "I got to look for somethin'." So I tried a couple of nights bein' a waiter on tables at a restaurant down on 59th Street that had these beautiful murals that some artist painted. I forgot who he was, and I can't remember the name of the place. They put me right up in the front part of the restaurant, and I didn't know shit about waitin' on tables for food. They wanted me to stay, but after two nights I decided I didn't like it particularly, so I didn't go back. Well, in the meantime this Prince Gene—the one that had worked with me in the balcony at the Howdy Club—he had accumulated a little money through the months there, 'cause he was very thrifty, man. He was runnin' an 11-room roomin' house on the side. So he figured he owed me a favor, and he said that he could get me a job at one of these tearooms they had up on 42nd Street and around in that area at the time. That was where they had these tea-leaf readers that would read your fortune. And Prince Gene knew this woman that was a reader at this place called the Wishing Cup Tea-room. So he went to this woman and told her that I was a reader friend of his from California who was lookin' for a place in New York to be a reader. And she told him, "Oh, that's good. The man who used to read here, he just died, dropped dead there in that booth just yesterday." So there was an openin'. Well, Gene knew all this, see, but I didn't.

12. THE WISHING CUP

I lay down and I cried the night before I went to work as a reader. The next mornin' I talked to God, and I said, "Look at me, God. I've wasted my whole life. I have seeked your path, and now where am I? What will I do?" I had nowhere to turn.

Becomin' a reader in the tearoom was my last straw. It's got to be the last straw. But it was either that or conform and cut my hair, and God knows what kinda job I would've got. So I thought, "Well, I can take anything to keep from comformin'."

These tearooms were all in the Fifth Avenue section—Broadway, 42nd Street East, 42nd Street West, up Fifth Avenue toward Macy's, and down in there they was scattered around. Goin' to the tearoom for readin's was very popular when they first opened. The readers made big money, or some of 'em did. But before the tearooms opened up there was people that would do readin's in their apartments, mostly readin' cards. And the way I got it sized up, this clique of lawyers decided they were gonna open up these tearooms, so they made it against the law for you to read cards in your own apartment. And after that people would write in and say that this one or that one was readin' cards, and they'd send a detective to trap 'em. And I often wondered how that all worked in there, because it seemed to all tie together.

But anyway, it was just a few days after I got back to New York in '45 that this Prince Gene took me down to the Wishing Cup Tearoom to see this woman about gettin' a job as a reader. They had these booths with a lattice between each one, and there was a reader in each one of these booths. Five readers in all. And we sat down at one of these booths, and the woman said,"That's the booth you'll sit in." I didn't have to do no demonstration or nothin'. She just took Gene's word for it that I was a reader. You know, she figured, "Well, if he says he's a reader, then he must be able to do it." But she said, "I can't tell you for sure now. I have to speak to the owner." So she spoke to the owner that night, and two days later I received a post card that said, "Come to work at three o'clock tomorrow."

Well, I got spruced up and went and had my manicure and got myself all clean, thinkin', you know, that was the secret of fortune-tellin' was good-manicured nails. I had a lot to learn. And the night before I went to the tea room I went to Prince Gene, and I said, "Man, can't you give me some pointers?" And he said, "Have you got nerve enough to say you're a reader?" He said, "If you've got nerve enough to say you're a reader and do it, you're a reader. If you haven't, then you can't do it." Well, I said, "You know dam' well I got nerve enough." He said, "Well I know you can do it. All you got to have is the opportunity." And he tells me, he says, "I always tell 'em that they'll travel more in the future than they have in the past, and blue is their favorite color, and they're very artistic." He says, "In other words, you flatter them a lot." But I knew from bein' in the Howdy

Club and watchin' him read fortunes there that he was the type that would read for people and they didn't come back to him. So I knew I had to be better than him. And I thought, "Well, there ain't but one way to do this. You got these people comin' to you, and you know you've gotta talk to 'em. You got to say somethin' that's gonna please 'em, make 'em feel happy inside." And I figured I was already psychic from bein' in that nightlife scene for so many years.

So that next day at three o'clock I went in, and the owner said, "You ready to go to work?" I said, "Yeah." So I got to the table. The owner's name was Peggy Fitzpatrick. She was a real Irish biddy. She was a lez. That's why she give me the job, I guess, 'cause she knew I was gay. But that first day when I come in, she says, "Here's this young lady here." So I sat down and read this gal's tea leaves. I had done seen tea leaf readers before, so I knew how it was done. I would take the tea leaves, and I would stir 'em around in the cup, and I'd turn it upside down and I'd let it drain in the saucer, let it settle. Tea leaves, if you're gonna read 'em you don't wanna read 'em just stirred up. You want 'em to set and draw up, so sometime you can grasp somethin' in there.

So this first girl I read, she jumped up and she said, "Oh you're wonderful! Now, you got this somewhere! I haven't heard this before." She said, "Will you be here tomorrow?" I said, "Yeah." She said, "Well, I'll send my sister." So right away people liked me. And she sent her sister, and her aunt come, and her mother, and her brothers and her uncle. People from all walks of life come into that tearoom, and I'd read their teacup.

But after that first night I said, "I'm tired." And Peggy said, "Oh, just relax and learn to say what comes into your mind." She says, "That's the best way. Don't worry or plan what you're gonna say." She would fill in as a tea reader and a fortune-teller sometime, but she didn't like it as a steady dish. Mostly she would just set all the people down and give out the tea, but she would read teacups when there was a crowd there and we had to get 'em out. 'Cause she was an old-time waitress, and she knew how to hustle them people for tips out there. And some of the readers would give her money to throw all the business their way. When I first started in the tearoom I had to sit there quite a while and learn how to do cross-stitch, and set idle. In those days I was lucky if I made 30 dollars a week.

There was a reader named Elsa that sat up in front, next to the street. And she was givin' this Peggy Fitzpatrick so much money every week. But she and I got along very well together. We never had any arguments or any bitchin' or nothin'. I used to just sit there and marvel, 'cause she'd pitch 'em out one right after another—bang, bang, bang, bang. That's how I learned to get the technique down. You see, when you first start to get into this tea-leaf readin' business you got to know how to set a person down and how to get 'em up—how to begin with 'em and how to end with 'em. You got to know how to start and when to stop it. And have it all under control, 'cause if you don't, you're in for trouble. You weren't supposed to take over 10 minutes with any of 'em, and less than that if you could. It took me a little while to get that wrinkle.

The young girls that come into the tearoom wanted to come over and see me, 'cause I was young lookin', and I looked nice and dressed nice, and they wanted to see what I had to say. After I started workin' in the tearoom I began to get sweatshirts and dye 'em a brilliant color, and I'd do cross-stitches and work Indian designs on 'em. In them days there wasn't no red shirts and things like that, all except for flannel nightshirts or unless you had one made. Anybody who put on a bright color was considered gay, *bang,* right away.

But in that tearoom I had to learn to rely on my psychic screen, and learn to say what I thought and what come to my mind. And I learned to get people who come from down on Wall Street. They was lookin' for numbers and tips and hints. I didn't know what it was all about, particularly, but I'd hear that certain ones worked on Wall Street and was interested in stocks. And then I learned that I could take that teacup, and I could hold it up here to my eye, like I was lookin' in it, and that way I could close my eyes and I could rest. And sometime I would look in the cup and I would see things, and then I learned to quote what was in my mind. And I used to quote numbers. I'd say, "Seven is up, and up is nine, and 21 is right on Tuesday," and things like that. And they would write them things down. And they would go back, and sometime they would get hunches from them things. I had a bunch of them Wall Street guys around my neck, man. They was really cheap as hell, too. They'd only wanna tip you a dime. So you had to learn to get rid of them dime tippers, man. Get them quarters or half a dollar, you know. You had to learn how to instinctively know them. And with them you would get a little better. You would get into more detail. 'Cause you only got a quarter out of every dollar that you took in, and then your tip.

So I learned, and I gradually began to make more money. By the time I stopped workin' as a reader there I 'magine I made 200 dollars a week, so I was makin' a lotta money for them people, man. That's why they put up with my shit. I'd leave in September and come down here to tend to the farm. And they'd tell me, "Well, when you come back somebody'll be in your place." But they never got nobody in my place. It was a hard rigamarole, baby. And you've got to learn it to learn it.

All this time I was doin' paintin' and drawin'. And when I got in the tearoom and started makin' some money I was able to buy some colors and some paper and some frames, and I learned how to stretch canvas. First I used watercolors, though, for quite a few years. And when I started readin' I left my old life behind. Too glad, man, I was. Good riddance of bad rubbish, really. 'Cause it was really low and degrading in a lot of ways. And I dropped all friends and everybody I knew. I didn't cultivate friends no more. I didn't make it my business to cultivate friends.

But I was paintin' like mad then, man. I'd go to work in that tea-room from three to 10, and then I'd go back home and light up a joint or two and go to work on the paintin' I had on the wall. I was paintin' scenes of ancient temples—Mayan—and some of the ancient civilizations, and some of the heads with the upswept hair. All kinda things. Beautiful paintin's.

It was just a little ol' room I was livin' in—five feet wide and nine feet long. 'Cause with my hair like it was, and my beard and all, they wouldn't let me in nice places. They'd say, "There's no vacancy," or "We just rented it," or "Gimme your number and I'll let you know somethin'." You know it was always pass-the-buck.

That was on 52nd Street where I lived at the time. That was when 52nd Street was jumpin' with Count Basie, Margaret Sullivan, Billie Holiday, Thelonious Monk. That was when bebop started. And a lotta these cats got high on speed—amphetamines. And there was an inhaler that come out at the time, and the musicians would take this benzedrine outta them inhalers and put it in their coffee and drink it. And they'd get so high they couldn't remember the notes they was s'posed to play, so they just made up somethin' else instead, and they called it bebop. That's how bebop was born.

I was always goin' to the museums in them days and lookin' at the latest shows. I'd go to the Metropolitan. And the Museum of Natural History became my hangout for many years. I learned a lot there. It was a very educational place. They was always showin' these films on tribal cultures and their dances and rituals, and I would go to see those. You could see all these races and all these tribes, and all these different styles and designs this tribe had, that tribe had. So it was interesting to see and learn. And when I wasn't workin' in the tearoom or in my room lit up high and workin' on a paintin', I was at the museums studyin' all these different cultures.

I tried to get some of my art in the galleries in New York, but I just couldn't ever get through. They wouldn't ever accept me. I was too bizarre for 'em. Sometime I even paid to get in galleries and group shows. I was in the Leon Tomler Gallery and another one on the East Side that Anna Dallas had. That Philip Pearlstein was in it—he's sellin' his work now. We was in a group show together. And I knocked on doors—advertisin' companies—tryin' to sell some work. They didn't want it. It was just...Well, it just wasn't like the average art.

Them newspaper and radio people knew me, man. 'Cause this Wishing Cup Tearoom was right down under Radio City, and some news people who worked for one of the networks come into the tearoom and said that they was with Harry Reasoner. They might've been lyin', I really don't know. But there was this photographer with 'em, and he took my picture where it looked like I'd jumped outta this big Radio City buildin' down onto this roof. I was wearin' some leotards, and my beard was braided up, and I had some kinda turban on, and had a beautiful pose. And they put that picture on the front page of this paper that came out in them days— the *Evening Journal* or somethin'. But that picture come out in the first edition, and then they pulled it. And then later I saw Morley Safer down in the streets, and he tried to laugh me outta the street. Him and that other one, the one that does that "On the Road" thing on the television news now—Charles Kuralt—would see me comin' and they'd jump back and hide. They really didn't wanna be bothered with me. They really wanted to ridicule me outta the fuckin' street, to tell you the truth, because I was comin' up with a completely new thing, man—the hair up, not down, the sewin' of the beard. And I had guts enough to do what I wanted to do, and they didn't like it. One of 'em made a remark about "You'll never get nowhere," or somethin' like that.

See, New York was not interested in new ideas, 'specially if they were that radical. That's why I don't like it anymore. And nowhere else is particularly interested in new ideas, either.

13. LEAVING THE CITY

My mother died in September of 1950, and I had to come back down here that fall to take care of the place. That's when I had to start comin' back every year and tendin' to the crops. By that time there were these two tenant-farmer families that worked on the farm, but I had to come back and tend to the peanuts and the cotton and get the corn up. And I would divide up the crops with them. They lived in a house up there and another one down there by the side of the road. And nobody lived here in this house while I was in New York. I just lived here four months out of the year, and I always had my own money when I come. It was very cheap to live here in those days, 'cause I'd do strict yogi diets and such as that, where you could live very economical. I didn't have no locks on the doors or nothin'. I got me some cement and I made this figure of Siva, the Hindu god of dance, on this thing kinda like a tombstone, and when I'd leave I'd put that out in front of the house. And I told these tenant farmers, I said, "If anybody walks by this thing while I'm gone they'll fall under a evil spell and drop dead." So the word got around back in here, and didn't nobody ever bother the place or come in the house while I was gone. I still got that Siva figure. It's out there back around on the other side of the house.

It wasn't until 1957 that I got my four acres. I was really entitled to about 60. There were six of us, brothers and sisters, and there was 374 acres. I wanted 60 acres up there on that side of the road that went down around and joined on the creek, but my brother Julius, the oldest one, told me, "You'll have to go to court to get it." He said, "I'll give you the house, the well, and four acres of land." And at that time, man, I couldn't see where no money was gonna come through my career, so I thought, "Well, it's a home and a place I can call my own. At least I can do what I want to there."

But I worked in the tearoom until I come back down here for good in '57. I developed a pretty good followin' at the Wishing Cup Tearoom, and after I'd been there for a while I was really the only reader there who could draw anybody to the place. I was havin' to handle all the business. That Elsa, who had been so popular for years by bribin' the hostess, she had lost track. And she was sittin' there just starin' at the cards.

But after my mother died I passed the word down here at home that I was a reader, and I began to pick up local business. So durin' those four months I was here I'd maybe get one or two or three a week, somethin' like that. And maybe one or two on Saturday and one or two on Sunday. And from that it just kep' growin' all through them years there. And finally, when I come home in 19 and 56, in September, I realized then that they was comin' pretty regular. I was gettin' four or five or six or seven a day. And I realized I could make as much here as I was in New York. So I thought, "Shit! Fuck New York! I don't need it no more."

But I went back anyway, in '57. And this old Wishing Cup Tea-room had closed. I don't know whether they lost their license or were sold or whatever happened, but it was closed. So I went over to this tearoom on 50th Street, the Gypsy Teakettle. It was across the corner from the Roxy Theater, upstairs over a bar run by black people, where they sold chitlins and Southern dinners and all such as that. I knew the hostess there, so I got a job as a reader. That was in January of '57. I immediately developed a following at the Gypsy Teakettle, but I only stayed there four or five months, 'cause on May the 26th I was sittin' in my room that night and this light came shinin' in the window. And somethin' just come over me, and that inner voice spoke to me and said, "Get up from here and go home. Leave this fuckin' city." So I packed my things and went and bought a one-way ticket on the train back to Georgia.

I was sick of New York anyway, to tell you the truth. It gets old after a while. I was glad to get out. Glad I had a place to get out to. I wouldn't be alive now if I hadn't.

14. BUILDING PASAQUAN

After my mother died and I had this place all to myself I started haulin' these rocks and stones outta the field and bricks from old houses and chimneys that had done been torn down, and I'd put 'em in piles in the woods around the house here. And to tell you the truth, I didn't even know what I was gon' do with 'em. I had in mind that I wanted to build somethin', but I didn't really know what. And it wasn't till I left New York and come back down here for good in '57 that I started buildin' on the place. I never had any overall plan. Everything was from day to day.

First I put up a fence out there by the side of the house, facin' the road. There was a young black guy who lived up the road here—D. W. Milner was his name—and I hired him to help me build it. I didn't know nothin' at the time about lines and line levels and all that shit. I just knew that I could see these designs in my mind, and these beautiful symbols—very weird. And I knew they represented the universe and its forces and the great powers that hold all of this planet here together. So I began to make these designs and symbols outta cement on these big round circles in wood. And D. W. would help me build up from the ground with these rocks and bricks I had done hauled in, and I'd set these big circle things in there. And when I started buildin' that fence I said, "I'm gon' build a serpent." 'Cause in the Indian cultures they mention of the serpent that was in the sky, and lightnin' struck her. Then she laid the three cosmic eggs, and the three islands of Mu was born in the Pacific Ocean. One 'rose, then another 'rose, then another 'rose, as this serpent laid these cosmic eggs. That's ancient Mu mythology that I read about in these books by Sir James Churchward.

So I was gon' build a serpent, but I really didn't know how to make a serpent, and I didn't make it right. I missed the serpent, but I got the fence. It was about 15 feet long, waist high. Some of them symbols on them circles was beautiful, though. I had the yin-and-yang, and the head with the hair all goin' up, and I had cactus plants drawn on some of 'em, 'cause I had known of the cactus in another life, in another person, when I lived among the Indians. But I found out it was a big mistake to put them designs on wood, man, 'cause they all rotted away inside. And anyway, the whole fence was crooked. So I left it up for a few years, and then sometime 'round '61 or '62 I tore it down.

I was experimentin', feelin', findin', learnin' somethin' I didn't know nothin' about. It was all trial and error, trial and error, trial and error. I made a lotta mistakes. That's how I learned a lotta things here. I'd make mistakes, and I'd do certain things to cover 'em up.

So D. W. dug up all these foundations we had put down under this first fence, and he said, "I'm goin' away to Chicago, but first I'm gon' help you get up this fence right. I promise that." So D. W.'s cousin Jimmy Milner and Jimmy's brother Estes come to work for me about that time. They weren't skilled at all, but I was payin' 'em, and I would figure it out. They would just do what I told 'em. I'd always say, "Well, I'm gon' do this," and automatically they would say, "I can do it," and would just go to doin' it. It was slow, but I was willin' to let 'em take it slow and let 'em learn. And that D. W., he could get the gist pretty quick. You know, if you're an artist and you've got somebody to execute your work and carry it out, and set the design and take it on after you make it, that's wonderful. You can go on to other things right away. Otherwise you got to keep your mind occupied on it.

That first fence I had out here, that I tore down, was crooked, but it still looked exotic, like a piece of weird sculpture, and had a wave to it. There was atoms and light prisms and all kinda weird stars and shapes and things to it. But I hadn't got down the technique to it yet. That was all in learnin'.

I learned a complete new system. But really it's not a new system. It's just what you call an ancient system. The ancients used it in their big murals and so forth and so on. So that's how I learned. But at the time it always seemed there was a good spirit right at my side who would say, "Well, that's right. This is right." And they would tell me that it was so many feet and that it was so many inches, and there was a design you wanted to go on there. So I'd add a little leverage onto each end of the mural—maybe six or seven inches—and put some kinda design. Then I'd have these big energy designs, or these whirls goin' 'round. That represents energy, and the forces they speak about in the Land of Mu. Well, for them I cut out the design of that whirl goin' 'round, and I made the pattern on a piece of roofin' felt, and I showed it to D. W. and Jimmy or Estes, and I said, "Here's that line. Now all you got to do is just take this here thing and put it up against the wall and draw this thing around it. Move it on over here. Don't never let it lap. Keep it right, and pull right into that form again, and you get the thing goin', you see." I simplified it for 'em. I broke it down. 'Cause it was just cold wet cement, and you didn't have too much time to ponder. You had to be set for what you was gon' do when you got there. You couldn't go there and start thinkin' what you're gon' do. You had to go there, and it had to be done. You only had about 30 minutes—40 at the most—to where it would be cuttin' right, and you had to move like hell. We put up that whole middle there in one wall in one day, man, and got the design on it. But I had to lay it out and line it up, and then cut the pattern. As I say, there were some very good spirits around here in them days. I've done all this work here through spirits guidin' me.

This is work that I had to pick up when I had time, because I found out that I couldn't run to the readin' table in the house here to tend to my customers, then go back and forth and work on these designs and these murals. Every time I'd get a new one started, I'd have to stop it to come inside and do readin's. So I started doin' somethin' that somebody else could do part of it and just let me do the design. And that way I was able to run out here and whip on a face right quick. 'Cause I love to just take a big piece of cement and make it come out as somethin'. I could just feel visions through them spirits, and I'd put 'em up on these walls that them Milner boys was buildin'— *bang, bang, bang, bang, bang*—and then it was there. So they built the basic walls, and all the lines I did, and all these designs and faces and heads with the hair goin' up. I would put them faces on there, and then after we got it I'd sit back and look at 'em, and I'd think, "Well, geez, I can see so-and-so's face in that one, and that one there is so-and-so." A lotta these faces that you see out here are people I useta know in New York—Tillie the Toiler, Clarence Hogue, Stella Dallas, Betty Boop—and some of 'em are of people that live around here nearby. D. W. Milner's in there, and my mother, and some other ones. So it was just the impressions them people made on me.

I didn't foresee nothin'. I thought, "What're you doin' this for?" But, man, it was just like a demon with me. I just said, "The spirit's gon' guide me here now." So I just followed the spirit, and this is what I come up with. I didn't use no special instruments or nothin'. I lined up all these walls with the eye, and I had no more idea what I was gon' put on 'em than the man in the moon. Although I knew I was gon' do somethin'. And after I got these walls put up, then I felt I had the world shut out.

There was a guy named Edwin Stephens that helped me with some of this here. He learned me about line levels and a plumb line and all that shit about linin' things up. I didn't know nothin' 'bout it. But he was a road worker—big machine operator—and he was workin' on the foundation for this road that goes by here, and that's how I met him. That was in about 1960, I remember, 'cause I had just bought a new Ford pickup truck at that time.

Stephens was a white guy, 'bout 55 years old, married, and had three kids. He was wiry and tough. I think he'd been on the chain gang, really. But he was very nice and sweet. He wasn't beautiful, but he wasn't bad-lookin' either. There was somethin' sexy about him. I had seen him out there workin' on the road, and he had come over to get clearance about some pines that was in the right-of-way on my land that had to be cut down for 'em to widen the road. So a few days later I drove by where he was workin', and I stopped to talk to him. I told him 'bout some pictures of my place that I had down yonder, and he said, "I'm gon' come down there and see 'em." So I said, "When you comin'?" And he said, "I'll be by there this afternoon."

So he come, and he swaggered down the walk. He looked lean and mean. He was very well hung—had a nice big prick hangin', and he let it show. He *wanted* you to see it. And I thought, "Look at this!" Everything turned out hunky. He was a real weird freak, man. So he was in the scene for a couple of years, and we was lovers. He'd go to work in different parts of the state, and then he'd come back down here for a while. He helped me lay these cinderblocks on the back part of the house that I added on, and he helped me put the sidin' on the house. He'd get these great big logs—that big around, man—from out in the woods. After they stripped 'em they were in seven-foot lengths. And I'd tell him how to carve 'em, and we used those on some of the walls and in the ceilin's some places. Course, I was payin' him for all this. After a while he gave up his job workin' on the roads down here and got a job in Baltimore, but he'd come back down here in the wintertime. He moved his family to Buena Vista for a while. They had a apartment there in town.

Stephens wanted to be a reader, and he thought he could learn it through me. And he kep' tellin' me, "Let me try! Let me try!" But I kep' puttin' him off, 'cause I knew that if he found out he couldn't do it, that would be the end of that. Durin' them days in the early '60s I useta take a plane and go to New York occasionally, and I'd have readin's lined up. I reckon I made about 20 trips up there in '60, '61, '62, and sometime he'd come up there on weekends when he was livin' in Baltimore. I'd be doin' readin's in private apartments, and he'd come along with me. I would line up them readin's through church secretaries up there and other people who knew people that wanted readin's. They was all black. Or maybe one out of a hundred was white. That was when I was still buildin' up a reputation, and a lotta the people I contacted and read for up there had relatives in the South. So anytime I'd read for one of them I'd tell 'em to write and tell their relatives about me and where I lived. And that way I could build up my business down here. 'Cause I never have done no advertisin' or even put up a sign that said I was a reader. It's all been through word of mouth.

But anyway, it finally come to the showdown between me and Stephens on one of them trips to New York, and I had to let him try it. So he tried it, and he couldn't make it. He realized he couldn't read, 'cause he wasn't psychic, and when he come back that was the end. So from then on out it was, you know, "Fuck you!" He thought since he knew me it'd rub off on him, I guess, but it didn't. I was a nervous wreck by the time that whole thing was over, man. That cured me from ever bein' in love again. So finally he moved his family away from here, and that was the end of it. Which I was glad of, really.

Me and these helpers I had worked on this place for 10 years before I started paintin' it. It was just the walls and columns and all these figures and designs and symbols drawn and cut on the cement. I hadn't decided on the colors yet. I didn't start paintin' 'em until after I went down to Mexico. I wanted to go down there to get some inspiration from them Indian cultures, man. So in 1965 I got a brand new Ford station wagon—the one I still got—and I was gon' drive it down to Mexico right away. But then I thought, "No, I'll get the Berlitz system and pick up all the Spanish I can before I go down there." So I fucked with that on and off for two years, and learned enough to say what I wanted to say and ask for what I wanted and so forth and so on. And in '67 I drove down to Mexico City. Nobody went with me. I went by myself.

When I got to Mexico City I checked in at the Hotel de la Reforma, and that's where I stayed the whole time I was down there. It was really a high-class hotel, and you couldn't get in with just anything on. So I was wearin' conventional two-piece suits and a sport shirt and a tie at the time, and I wore a big purple taffeta turban that I made. You could wear it as a turban or you could wear it as a sari. I didn't meet nobody while I was down there. I didn't communicate at all, except in the place where I went to eat, and with one guide I used for one day, and that's all. I'd go to the movies in the daytime, and I went out there to the Hotel Prado, where they've got that great big old Diego Rivera mural. But I had seen that already, years before in *Life* magazine. Nothin' was new down there. It was all somethin' I had seen before. But it was a challenge to run off on my own by myself. I never had been off on a trip like that by myself. I'd like for somebody to've been with me, though. I think I would've enjoyed it more that way.

I went all over them ruins, man. I caught a airplane and flew up over Guatemala and Yucatan and all such as that. It was a group thing. You paid 65 dollars and you went for a day tour. So I saw some of them temples. And I saw the Museum of Archaeology in Mexico City. But I had already seen them ruins from the travelogues and travel adventure films, and it was really more interesting to see 'em on the screen than it was to be there.

I really oughtta've stayed down there longer, though. If I'd had someone with me I would've. But I found out I couldn't go out in the street at night by myself. And I'd seen them Mexicans and Spanish-speakin' people in New York, so I knew their actions, their types, their ways. 'Cause they've got the same fuckin' thing there as they do in New York—them hipsters, them goofers, them hangers-on, and what-have-you.

So after I had been in Mexico City for about 19 days I went up on the roof of that Hotel de la Reforma durin' a lightnin' storm one night, and I looked up at that big snowcapped volcano and all the lightnin', and the spirit told me, "Okay, now you've got what you came for." So the next day I got in my station wagon and drove back here. And when I come back I was fully converted to the Indian way of life—thoughts, beliefs, heart, mind, body, soul, spirit, everything. So that's when I went into makin' beads and learnin' about tapestries, and I started puttin' the paint on these walls here then.

I kep' addin' on to the place in those years after I come back from Mexico, and paintin' as I went along. I tried lettin' my helpers do it.

I said, "Paint that." I said, "There's a design and a pattern to it." But they couldn't pick this out. They could look, but they couldn't see if it was s'posed to be red here, yellow there, and so forth and so on. So I had to tell 'em what colors to put and where to put 'em.

There are symbols from all kinda ancient cultures on them walls and temples, man—American Indian, Chinese, Japanese, African. Some of them symbols represent energy and space and unknown things that we can't see but that's in the air around us. 'Cause there's invisible matter that's goin' through our bodies all the time that we can't see. Some of these symbols represent magnetic fields that's travellin' out there, and some of 'em represent energy givin' force out in space, sendin' it all out in compact colors and designs and patterns—although they would be microscopic. Some of 'em represent the globe—the planet earth—and Mars, Jupiter, Saturn, and so forth and so on. And the sun. And shootin' stars and spaceships, and the atom that they have to take outta the air to run them ships. Some of them big round designs represent some ancient court where I was a court jester in another life, or a medicine man among a great tribe in the past.

As I say, some of them heads represent people that I have known. And there's all kinda figures in erotic poses. I've even got two dudes from Hell's Angels on one of them walls. I was doin' them heads, and I hadn't decided who they was gon' be yet. And I come inside to wait for the cement to harden up a little bit more, and I saw a news thing on the television about the Hell's Angels. There was two of 'em that caught my fancy, so when I come back out to put the finishin' touches on them heads I put their looks on 'em.

Them figures on them big totems are mythological figures from the Land of Mu. That's the natural image of man, bein' his true self, growin' his beard, his hair long, and learnin' the art of it, takin' care of it. The natural man is not like these other people that you see runnin' around in this society today, man, 'cause they're just what you call "curriculum people." They do just like somebody says for 'em to do. And all these designs all around them faces on them totems represent a complete elastic suit that puts pressure on the right parts of the body, so that man can control levitation of his body and be lifted up and keep himself away from the pull of gravity, so he can act normally out yonder in space. Man has that power in his body and don't know it. Them suits haven't been developed yet, but I've seen 'em in visions that the spirit has shown to me. They'll be pressurized, and they're all drawn together with elastic bands, and there's a frame thing that comes in here and covers up part of his face, and there's glass over his eyes so he can see out of it. It'll be air-conditioned and everything.

That big pagoda out on the corner there with that stairway goin' up to it in a big sweepin' curve—that sits over top of the old well that was here before my mother bought this place in the '20s. It'll be a healin' well someday, after I'm dead and gone, and people'll come here from all over to be psychosomatically healed. I built that pagoda over it in about '63, '64.

There was a mood for change in the '60s, when I was buildin' all this. And I was the symbol of this change. But I've been denied it, 'cause I was too bold and brazen. I could've had a cult goin' here, man, but the people that I saw comin' to me that I had to put up with to start it, I just didn't feel like puttin' up with 'em. I always had my work as a psychic reader to fall back on, to make some bread. If I had to use them people to get a little scratch from 'em to maneuver and live on, it would've been difficult. There was a few long-haired kids that started showin' up here at the end of the '60s when everything was jumpin' around. The rich kids from Columbus come out, and a dance class come out. They was more or less middle-class or rich kids. The whole clique was just strictly conformist. Rednecks. That's all. They was curious and wanted to know, but I had sense enough to know that if I had accepted them bastards and took up a little time with 'em, they would've tried to rip me off or rob me or bump me off. But some of 'em would come out, so I'd let 'em in, and I talked to 'em in gutter language and so forth.

When I first come back down here from New York I read about Socrates and dug what happened to him, man. And that was two thousand years ago. So my mind said, "Concentrate on your work and let things alone. I'll show you what to do and how to do." That's why I've not seeked a following, 'cause I knew they'd tell me I was tryin' to corrupt their youth. And besides, I can't be out there greetin' people all the time. I got to make bread, man. But sometime when them kids come out I'd talk with 'em and jive along with 'em—you know, whatever the occasion called for. One of 'em brought a pistol one time and pulled it out. I said, "Put that fuckin' pistol in your pocket." I said, "You'll shoot your fuckin' brains out with it." And he put it up. But I knew they was bad, and I knew if I didn't take up some time with 'em they was liable to cause trouble. They thought I was gay, I guess. But youths never appealed to me.

Some freaks from up there at that Legionnaire's hall they got out there on Victory Drive in Columbus come out here one time. I don't know if they was soldiers from Fort Benning or what. I think they was. And they come around to the front door, and I wouldn't let 'em in. So they started yellin'. They said, "You god dam' gook!" Well, "gook" is an expression them military people use for Vietnamese and Orientals, you know. And that was when the Vietnam war was on. And they were sayin', "We'll kill you!" and all such shit as that. Well, I just looked at 'em through the window, and then they run out there and tried to pull them metal fringes offa them murals on that front wall, and they must've cut their hands on 'em, 'cause I went out there later and there was blood on 'em. But after a little while they drove away. I stayed in the house. I knew they would've jumped me if I had gone out there. I figured they might even have a gun, and I was all by myself. That was before I even had my dogs. But it was right after that that I got them dogs, 'cause I figured I better have some protection, man, if I wanted to stay alive.

That big Fort Benning army base is just a few miles away, man, and you can hear 'em havin' target practice, shootin' off them big guns and so forth and so on. Them helicopters are always flyin' over and circlin' the place. I think they bring the top brass from Washington over to show 'em my place whenever they come down to the base. And caravans of soldiers come by on maneuvers on the road out here. That base creates much noise and bad viberations, man. *Any*thing military gives me bad viberations.

Several years ago they was talkin' about expandin' Fort Benning all the way out here, and if they did that they'd take this place from me. When I first heard about that it really jarred me. I reckon it was about 10 years ago when that started. There was a meetin' about it in the gym at the high school in Buena Vista, and a buncha them officers came to it. I went in my Indian regalia, and when I walked in I saw the flagpole in there, but it didn't have no flag on it, and right away I knew somethin' was wrong there. I said to myself, "If you can't turn this thing around, man, then you ain't what you said you are." So I dead-eyed them officers all through that meetin', man. One of 'em— he was a captain or some kinda shit—he got up and said all the land they already had was too swampy to do trainin' on it, so they needed more land. The people out here in the country knew what it was all about, 'cause they remembered what happened back around the Depression years, when they first started Fort Benning. I talked to some of 'em, and they told me about how the soldiers came around with guns and kicked 'em outta their houses and off their land before they could even get their crops in. The Army took their land and destroyed their crops, and that just shows you how wasteful the Army is, man. I'd never given a thought to any of that until this happened. Man, it just pulled my sail right down. I think the government could be concerned about destroyin' this place, 'cause I claim it'll be a religious center some day. Someday people are gonna see the light and start to be their natural selves. But some people were delighted when they heard about this Fort Benning thing, 'cause they thought it would destroy me. They thought, "Man, this place is gon' be gone now." What people don't understand, they try to tear down. But there ain't nothin' in the papers about it the last few years, so I don't know what's gon' happen.

I built this place to have somethin' to identify with, 'cause there's nothin' I see in this society that I identify with or desire to emulate. Here I can be in my own world, with my temples and designs and the spirit of God. I can have my own spirits and my own thoughts. I don't have nothin' against other people and their beliefs. I'm not askin' anybody to do my way or be my way, although when I'm gone they'll follow like night follows day. 'Cause Pasaquoyanism is the next religion that's gon' come on the scene, man. I don't know who it'll be, but somebody's gon' pick it up. It may get started before I depart. You can't tell. And it may not come in my time, but somewhere along the fuckin' line somebody's gon' come along like me, who's gon' rebel, and there's gon' be others.

I was sent here to bring new styles, new ways of carin' for the body, the arts of the hair and the beard, and adornment of the body, as it was once upon a time in the days of the ancients, the Assyrians, the Mayans, the Olmecs, the Egyptians, the people of Atlantis and Mu. I wanna prove to society that even though I've been ostracized all my life, I have good qualities and good potential. I built this place just to prove that I could do it—to prove it to my own self, really. And I wanted to prove that I do have some ability and imagination, and can be innovative for the society if given a chance. Well, anyway, I keep on tryin'. I can't prove anything to the world, but it'll come to the fore when I'm dead and gone. 'Cause I was sent here as a prophet. But I'm a prophet without honor in his own land.

Sometime I get discouraged and ask God to show me a vision to let me know I'm on the right path. 'Cause I have a psychic screen in the back of my head, and when I lay down and close my eyes I watch that screen and I look for things. Sometime I lay there and I look and look, and nothin' don't come. Sometime I stay there and I look, and I begin to see these heads with this hair on 'em, goin' up. And sometime I'll see all these atoms and particles swirlin' around in front of me, and they'll come together and materialize into a body right before my eyes. I'll see these people flyin' through the air in strange suits, and they'll be sittin' on a thing that looks like a little lever.

You'll see that I have a lotta these perspective paintin's out here on these walls, with the road goin' off in the distance to the horizon. That's depth and perspective, which is a very important thing for an artist to learn, man. And your work ain't gon' have depth and perspective unless you live 'em in your life. So that road in them paintin's represents perspective—goin' off into the future toward the sun, like I did as a young lad. It's a long, long road out there, if you'll just reach out there and get on with it.

There's always somethin' over the hill.

15. POOR MAN'S PSYCHIATRIST

 could've built more of these temples and pagodas if I had been able to devote all of my time to it like I wanted to. But I've never been able to get in with any of them people that run the art world, man. That clique never would accept me, and I couldn't ever make a livin' by sellin' my work. So I've always had to go back to that table and that deck of cards and put up with them people that come here for readin's. I'm 77 years old now, and I'd like to retire from it, really. 'Cause goin' back and forth from my work out there on my beautiful temples into that front room with them people, that gets mighty old after a while. It's from one world to another.

These people that come here for readin's, I break it all down to 'em. They're puzzled and all in a whirl. They don't know *this,* they don't know *that.* And I just break it all down into a few common words of sense. And they understand that. What I am, really, is a poor man's psychiatrist. I've even had psychiatrists come to me for readin's. And

I listened to what they had to say, then I thought to myself, "My God! No wonder the people is fucked up!" 'Cause them psychiatrists were in the same trap as these people they were tryin' to show how to elude it: that *love* trap. Everybody's lookin' for love. But if you can't find happiness in this world except through somebody else, besides God above, then you're in trouble. 'Cause that love is like a bird. It's here today and gone tomorrow. It flies out the window like a fuckin' bird, man. Very quick: *bang,* and they're gone. And some people get hung up in all that shit. And when their bubble busts and their ego goes down, it really is a blow to a lot of 'em. They can't take it, man. They have nervous breakdowns and all that shit. I tell you, that "love" is a word that should be abolished from the language, and it oughtta be replaced with "respect" instead.

But when most of them people come in that front door I can look at their faces and see that somethin's wrong. There's no happy expression there, and you know somebody's givin' 'em hell to cause that. Mostly what I do is just listen to their story, and I take it from there. And I always tell 'em they're gonna do better. That's the main thing they wanna hear, because when they come to a person like me, they're down at the bottom of the ladder. They don't know whether they're comin' or goin' or what's gonna happen. So you have to say the right things to lift their spirits. I've asked some of 'em, I'll say, "What the fuck you come here so much for? Don't you get tired of comin' here?" And they say, "Oh, I always feel better when I leave you." So I must be doin' 'em some good.

I just add up and put two and two together. I get into the situation right away. A lotta readers, oh, they talk and talk and talk and talk, and they ain't ever got to the essence of the matter. You got to be able to get right in there. I call it "gettin' in to the bone." Right to the essence of what the problem is. And then you explain it to 'em.

It's amazing how people get mixed up in these love affairs they can't understand. They come in here and say, "How come he left me?" Or "How come she done this?" And I say, "Well, it's a woman or a man—one of the two. If he busted it up he's got another woman." Well, at first they can't seem to fathom that, although after you talk to 'em they find out they know all about it. Some of 'em just can't get it through their heads that somebody could drop them for somebody else.

Men have a habit of gettin' goin' with a woman, and they give 'em money and so forth, and then they say, "Well, I'm gon' test this bitch and see if she'll help me. I been helpin' her." So they generally come up and borrow a hundred or two-hundred, or as much as they can get. And then she'll start to taper off from it, and she'll go lookin' for another man to start doin' the same thing with. And these men can't get it through their head how a woman'll do that after they've done so much for 'em. They'll say, "I don't wanna give her up. I got too much invested in her." I say, "What do you mean, 'invested in her'?" And they'll say, "All the money I been givin' her. I done bought her furniture, bought her a car and all such shit as that." And I say, "Well, you was just a dam' fool."

You have to speak very plain to 'em, and in common language. I speak very filthy to 'em sometime. They seem to like it. Sometime I'll say to a woman, "I hope I'm not offendin' you with some of these words I'm sayin'." And they'll usually say, "Oh, no. I appreciate it." Some woman that was here the other day, she said, "I just can't understand my son leavin' his wife and gone down there with that other woman." I said, "You don't understand it? She's got better pussy than that one's got." I said, "That's what it is. If a man leaves a woman and don't wanna fuck her no more, he's found somethin' else he wants to fuck better. 'Cause pussy gets stale." And she said, "Well, I never thought of it like that." So I said, "Well, give it a thought."

I look for little signs about 'em when they come in here, like if there's a mark on that ring finger on the left hand. That ring makes a mark on the finger, and if a woman takes off a wedding ring, that's a sign that she wants a divorce, or that she's not too happy with her marriage. So if a woman comes in here, and I don't see that left hand, I say to 'em, "Cut the cards with your left hand." And that gives you a good chance to look at that finger. So I look at 'em, and if they got the ring over here on this other hand, that means they're lookin' for a husband. Or some of 'em'll take the ring off just to confuse you, and you don't know whether they're divorced, separated or what. But I've found out that with them I can just say that I see two marriages—marriage, then divorce, then another marriage. Or marriage and divorce and two or three or four more marriages. And it generally fits in.

This girl came in here the other day, and she was wonderin' about her boyfriend. She said, "You know how it is when you're in love." And I said, "Honey, fuck that love." I said, "Never mind. You just take this attitude in your head: You've got a boyfriend. He comes around, and you get you a little once in a while." I said, "Think about him when he's there. When he ain't there, don't start worryin' about him." But she wants him to marry her, man. Shit, it'll be the sorriest day of her life. I says, "Is he cheap?" She says, "Very cheap." So I said, "Well, if you married him he'd be just that much cheaper, 'cause he knows you're makin' your bread." The ones that's not married, they always want a husband—someone to take care of and look after 'em. I guess that's women's prerogative.

The women that's been married for a while, though, they love to hear their husband is gon' die. They *love* to be told that. I'm tellin' you, it's just a disgrace when you think about it. They come in here, and I fiddle along with 'em, and I look at 'em, and I think, "Well, this bitch ain't happy with what she's got." So I'll say, "Have you got any insurance on your husband? Keep it paid, honey. He ain't gon' live very long." And sometime they'll drop a tear. They'll try to act like they're cryin', then they say, "Ooooh, I don't want my husband to die! And I say, "Why, you're a dam' liar! You do want him to die! You wanna get that insurance money." Well, then they say, "Well, I had thought about it."

When you're in this business you got to learn to say what's on your mind, and after you do it for a while, nine times outta ten it's right. Sometime you'll say to 'em, "So-and-so and so-and-so," and they'll say, "Aw, that couldn't happen to me!" And I'll say, "Dearie, you just wait and see. You'll see it happen." And a lotta times it happens. I've told women their husbands are gon' die on a certain day, a certain date, and shit, they'd die on that date, man! And that's like hittin' a number, man. 'Cause then all their friends come, wantin' to know when their husbands are gon' die.

I like it when I get up in the morning and have eight or nine or ten cars outside the gates there waitin' to be read. Some of 'em come before the sun even comes up. That's generally on Saturday or Sunday. Durin' the week it's slower, but then some weekdays it picks up.

Ninety-nine per cent of my business is black. I have a good rapport with 'em. I flinch when I see white ones comin', man. 'Cause most of them are a pain in the fuckin' ass. You ask 'em a question, and they say, "I didn't come for me to tell you. I come for you to tell me." And when that happens, my thought is to get the money and get it as quick as I can and get their ass out. So I just go through a line o' shit with 'em: "I see travel for you. You'll go to Mexico," or "Your aunt's gon' die," or some kinda shit like that. And you just give 'em the boo-boo-boo, and they're gone. They give me that money, and sometime I know they're not satisfied. I feel sorry for 'em, really. But I don't send for 'em, and I don't advertise. They come lookin' for me. So I let it stay that way.

With the blacks I take a different approach. When they sit down, I say, "What's your problem?" Now, these that's got these wigs on and wanna be like the whites, they're very difficult. But the other ones'll tell you what's on their mind. And I just set there and listen to what they've got to say, and analyze it for 'em, and tell 'em the situation—what is what. I don't give 'em a long time, maybe ten minutes. Sometime fifteen. And they seem to go away very happy.

The blacks always say, "I want *help*. Help my luck. Help get me outta this thing I'm in." You know, blacks—and whites, too—they go out on credit too much. They don't think about how much money they're makin' and how to spend it. Anybody'll sell 'em some credit, they grab it. And whites are the same way. They'll say, "Oh, I can't hold no money! Somethin' must be wrong." And I say, "How the hell can you hold money when you owe everything you make?" I say, "Time you get it, you got to pay somebody there, so there's none left for you." I say, "You have to catch up your debts and buy for cash, and that way you'll be able to hold a little money."

But to tell you the truth, with that readin' it's got to where it's just the same shit over and over and over and over and over and over and over. I may vary it a little bit, or speak a little differently, but otherwise it's more or less the same. But them people always tell me that it's not what I say, it's how I say it.

16. THE LONE PASAQUOYAN IN THE NEW SOUTH AND THE MODERN WORLD

)reckon it was along about 1974 or '75 that this Herbert Hemphill come to see me. He's this big art collector in New York. I believe he's from Columbus originally. He bought a painting from me. Of course he didn't wanna pay too much for it. And then it wasn't too long after that that these people from the Georgia Council for the Arts come out and took my picture and put it in this book called "Missing Pieces," and they took a film of me talkin' 'bout the arts of the hair and the beard and all, and doin' my rituals out there on that dance platform. There was a lotta other folk artists in the book and in the film, too. They really only had just a little bit in there about me.

So, after they did that film and that book, they wrote me a letter, the Council for the Arts did, and they said I was invited to some kinda folk art thing they was havin' in Washington at the Library of Congress. There was gon' be a group of us, it said, and that we were going on a plane, and to be in Atlanta at 11 o'clock in the waitin' room at the airport there. This was in the winter, in 1977, I think it was. 'Cause it was after Carter come in. And it was cold in Washington.

So I got to the airport there, and they all got there ahead of me. The Reverend Finster was there. He's a preacher and a artist. He knows how to hustle them paintings, man, I'll say that for him. But he was there, and Mrs. Busbee was there—the wife of the Governor of Georgia. And several of them people from that Georgia Council for the Arts. So we all met in this room there at the Atlanta airport. Some of 'em looked a little surprised when I walked in there, man. I had on my Indian regalia. They must've thought the Indians had done took the country back over. But when we marched out to the plane it was in a procession. Mrs. Busbee had me by the right arm, or she had her arm around my shoulder. And the Reverend Finster was on the other side of her. And he was blowin' a harp, and I was beatin' on my African talkin' drum and chantin' at the same time, as we walked on out to the plane. I think Mrs. Busbee was really kinda startled.

I was sittin' next to Reverend Finster on the plane. Man, he started talkin' when we got on, and he never stopped! You couldn't get a word in. You could just once in a while ask a question. He's just like a speed freak, man. So somethin' happened, and we couldn't land in Washington. We had to go to Baltimore. I don't know whether it was a ruse to hold back until the main events went on before they presented me—I have a feelin' that's what it was. But anyway, I helt onto the Reverend Finster and kep' him with me. He had never even been in a city before, I don't think. And we was in the last taxi outta that airport. So we had to ride in a taxi all the way to Washington from Baltimore. So we went to the Library of Congress, and there was this big party goin' on, and they was all around the table eatin'. But I didn't go in there, because I didn't wanna get caught in there, and I didn't feel like it.

They wanted to take us through the Library of Congress on a tour, but I didn't go through the whole thing with 'em. The first thing they showed us was this great big Bible that was very old. They had it in this glass case so nobody could touch it. And I said, "There's the book that brought slavery into the world!" 'Cause that Bible has always been used to keep people ignorant, and to keep man from thinkin' for his own self. The rich has always used it to keep the poor people all downtrodden. And them people looked at me, and some of 'em laughed kinda nervously like they was embarrassed. But didn't none of 'em say anything. So I decided I wouldn't go on the rest of that tour.

So after that I get my drum, and I walk up from the main floor in the Library of Congress, these windin' stairs that go up about the height of 18 feet. I had my drum, so I decided I was gonna go up there and do a chant. I was really gonna lay Congress *out,* I'll tell you that. I was on the warpath. And I just became inspired. I was still kinda high from smokin' this good stuff I had before leavin' home that day. And I wanted to do a number, so I started into it. I beat down on the drum, and I give a big war yell, a shaman yell. And all of a sudden this guard runs up and says, *"Oh! Ssshhh! You can't do that up here! You can't do that up here!"*

But shit, man, they brought me up yonder to Washington and all, but nothin' ever did come out of it. Them people still won't buy my art. At first I thought all this attention might lead to somethin', but it never did. I always wound up back at the table and that deck of cards, man. And I reckon I'm gon' have to keep up with that till I die. This fuckin' society we got here don't appreciate my art and my theories on the hair and the beard and all. But just you wait. When I'm dead and gone they'll follow like night follows day.

* * *

The other mornin' the sheriff come out here. Scotty come in the house and said, "The sheriff wants to see you." And I thought, "Oh, my God, what's this?" So I wrap a towel around me and go out the back door, and I ask him what he wants. And he says, "Well, first I wanna ask for your vote in the primary." And I says, "Well, you got it." And he says, "And second, ex-President Carter called and said he wanted to come and see your place."

That was Thursday. So, the next day Jimmy and Rosalynn and Amy flew up in their plane to the airport down there, and the sheriff escorted 'em out here with his four bodyguards. So Jimmy said, "Well, show us around." So they got out of their cars, and I looked at them secret service men, and I said to Jimmy, I said, "Man, you must wish you'd never been President, to have all this followin' you all the time." And he said, "Oh, they leave us alone when we ask 'em to." I didn't ever hear him tell 'em to leave us alone, but they didn't follow us the whole time they was here. When we got right outside the front door I looked right at them bodyguards, and I said, "Now, any of you that's got any bad viberations better not come in this house, 'cause my dogs can pick up on them viberations, and they'll tear into you if they're bad." 'Cause I could look at them protectors and tell they was a little hostile. I could tell they was thinkin', "What the fuck is this? Who is this?" You know. So they stayed behind when we went in the house.

But I took the Carters around through the place, and I gave 'em a few details about Pasaquoyanism and so forth. And I said a few words to him about why he got beat outta the White House that last time. I told him that Reagan's got just what this country wants: a good head o' hair and a mean line o' talk. And I asked him why he didn't do more things when he was in the seat of power. But I said, "You found out, I 'magine, that you can't do what you wanna do when you get in there."

You know, Jimmy come here to see me years ago, before he ever run for office. Before he run for State Senator or Governor or anything. Burton White brought him out here. He had the Ford dealership in Buena Vista at the time, and he knew the Carters. And Carter was lookin' for somebody that could talk up votes for him and push him on. So this Burton White was a wheel in the church, and he always managed the cancer fund drive. He was up in the social strata. So he brought Carter out here. This was right after he got outta the Navy. And he said, "This is a guy from down in the country here, and he's got some very big ambitions and ideas."

So I looked at him. All stoop-shouldered. And he says, "How come you do so many things?" And I said, "Well, that's what life is for— to learn about a lotta things." I said, "Don't let your mind get locked. You have to keep your psyche open, like a child, 'cause it's always out there to learn." I was givin' readin's for two dollars in them days, but he didn't wanna spend no money. So I finally just told him, I said, "I see great success for you. Go ahead and keep your mind and follow your plans and do what God tells you. Just pursue what you're after, and you'll accomplish it."

EOM's father,
Julius Martin, circa 1905

EOM's mother,
Lydia Pearl Story Martin, circa 1905

The pre-Pasaquoyan Eddie Martin
on a rooftop in Pontiac, Michigan, 1928.

Later, on the same rooftop, Eddie in drag, 1928.

St. EOM steps out,
demonstrating an exotic
Pasaquoyan ritual dance
on a New York City
rooftop, circa 1945.

St. EOM with a friend, New York City, circa 1948.

Studio portrait of St. EOM, New York City, circa 1950.

St. EOM's booth at an arts and crafts exhibition in New York City, circa 1952.

St. EOM studies the cards at the reading table in the front room at Pasaquan, 1959.

St. EOM embellishes one of the cement figures he created for the original front wall, later demolished, at Pasaquan.

This cement relief disc is the only portion of Pasaquan's original front wall that survived. It is now incorporated into one of the compound's side walls.

As the original Pasaquan compound took shape during the late 1950s, St. EOM posed proudly with his new creation. At right St. EOM holds over his face one of the masks to be incorporated into one of the compound's walls.

St. EOM at home, late 1950s and early 1960s.

St. EOM shows off some of his more unusual homemade headgear at Pasaquan, circa 1979.

The Pasaquoyan in a prayerful pose in his reading room, circa 1978.

Scotty Steward at Pasaquan after St. EOM's death, 1986. Photograph by Roger Manley.

St. EOM's funeral, April 17, 1986, Buena Vista, Georgia. Photograph by Tom Patterson.

17. GLEN ALTA REVISITED

One summer evening in 1984 not long before sunset, as the Marion County countryside was cooling off, I asked St. EOM if we could go and take a look at Glen Alta, the long-abandoned hamlet where he spent his childhood and early youth.

"There ain't nothin' there no more but the railroad track and three or four deserted little buildin's and a dirt road goin' through," he said. "Ain't nobody lived over there for years."

When I said that I would still like to see what was left of the place, the Pasaquoyan agreed to show me, and we got into my car and drove the eight miles of state and county road that took us to the forgotten corner of backwoods Georgia where Eddie Martin grew up. It's a few hundred yards off the nearest paved highway, on a huge tract of land now privately owned by a timber and pulpwood company, as Eddie explained to me.

As we turned off the highway, Eddie was bitching righteously about what had become of this area in the past half-century: "They done let these fuckin' forests here get in the stock market, man. What does the stock market care for the real benefit or welfare of anything except their stocks? They destroyed these woods that useta be here. I come out here one afternoon when they was burnin' and cuttin' all those trees. Man, about 50 rattlesnakes was gettin' out from there, comin' across the road! I just stopped the truck and let 'em get by in front of me, and then drove on. Some big corporation was destroyin' their habitat, and they was really hustlin' to get outta there."

I parked the car near the main road, and we got out and followed a narrow dirt alleyway down a gradual slope into the slash pine forest, ignoring the "POSTED: DO NOT ENTER" signs. Within minutes we arrived at what had once been the heart of Glen Alta, where the old road crossed the tracks on which, as a child, Eddie had watched the passenger trains go by en route between the big cities. There wasn't much to be seen here now but eroded red clay and kudzu and pine trees, with three or four abandoned wooden structures on either side of the railroad track. Eddie toured me through the site, describing matter-of-factly and with little trace of nostalgia what the landscape had looked like in this place more than 60 years ago, and elaborating now and then on his previous stories of what life had been like here in the old days.

"That was the store," he pointed out a rectangular wood frame building with a rusty tin roof. "The man who rented the store from Old Man Hatcher lived in an apartment in back of it. A blacksmith shop was sittin' right here under this oak tree."

Indicating a deserted house about 30 yards away in the shadows, he said, "The sawmill man lived over there. He had it pretty good, 'cause he made money even when the crops was failin'. But everybody else was a victim of the system, just like they are today. The sawmill man had all this money to buy hired hands to run his plows. Paid 'em five dollars a week. And you know what they lived on? Middlin' meat, gravy, biscuits and cornbread. It was just about the same thing as slavery."

We crossed the tracks and headed on up a hill, following the parched

246

red clay swath through the jungle of pines and kudzu. Eddie pointed out the overgrown remains of the one-room schoolhouse he attended during his childhood. Then he stopped near the crest of the hill at a tumbledown shack almost covered with kudzu vines.

"This is the house I lived in for the first 14 and a half years of my life," he told me. "We got our water from a spring that was just over the hill there, and there was spring water runnin' all down in through here. My mother useta wash clothes over there. There was an old sweetgum tree right there, and across the road there were all these great big old beautiful pines. So I'd stand here on this bank and look at these tall, graceful trees."

We continued along the little-used road, approaching the fields where Eddie and his father and his brothers had toiled for the estate's former owner, and Eddie said, "But I tell ya, I was only too glad to leave this place."

The roadway faded out into blackberry and honeysuckle not far past the old Martin homeplace, and we turned around, heading back toward the railroad tracks. We walked in silence for a while. An early evening birdsong occasionally broke the stillness of the approaching dusk. Then the Pasaquoyan began to wax reflective.

"You know, people are always sayin' to me, 'Oh, you must've had an interesting life!' Well, in a way I guess it was pretty interesting. But sometime I look back on it and I think, 'Aw, man, it was all a lotta shit. Just scufflin' to make a livin'.' It's lucky that I even survived and didn't ever get hooked on junk or nothin'. Sometime I think about it, and I say to myself, 'Jesus Christ! What a screwy life!' But I lived through it, and I'm still here, so I guess it had to be."

As we reached the bottom of the hill we stopped at the railroad, and Eddie looked down the tracks toward the setting sun. "I reckon all them people I useta know in New York are all dead now. Betty Boop and some of them others I got painted on the walls at my place, I don't know about them. There might be some of 'em still alive. I've had some dreams lately 'bout them people back in them days, so maybe I'll hear somethin' from one of 'em."

After a thoughtful pause, he said, "I had a dream the other night where I was on a subway train, and some guy who was with me said, 'I'm gon' show you how to drive this thing.' One of my dead brothers was in that dream, too. He come up to me on the train and said, 'Have you got a ticket?' And I said, 'He's gon' learn me how to drive it.' That's when I woke up. But I was thinkin' about that dream later, and I thought the ticket might be the symbol of death. I'm gettin' old now, you know, so I'm lookin' for the sign or the symbol. I think it's comin' before too long."

We crossed the tracks and began heading back to my car. Eddie was saying, "I don't get much charm outta life any more. I see too many things here that needs to be changed, and there's no way of changin' 'em. I'd like to see this fuckin' country take a new direction, man, and turn back to the Truth, and to nature and the earth. Someday man's gon' get sick of all this shit that he's goofed up around him here. Evolution's gon' catch up to him, if nothin' else. But I know somethin's got to give one day. The people in this society better start lookin' back to this earth, and gettin' these rivers and lakes clean, with fish back in 'em and jumpin', and people livin' in the woods again. Otherwise these cities is gon' bring it down on all of us. They're talkin' 'bout the greenhouse effect now, from all this pollution and shit that man has done put up in the air. But you can't be a natural person in this society, man. They'll ostracize the shit out of you every way they can. I know. This fuckin' phony shit that we got today, man, if it ain't 'bout to crush me. To tell you the truth, it's got to the point where every night when I lay down to go to sleep I hope and pray to God in heaven that I'll die. I just wanna pass out and be gone, make the change. I don't wanna linger and suffer."

St. EOM had had enough of the outside world for one afternoon. We got into my car and drove back to Pasaquan.

18. FINAL ACT

After his last visit to the ghost village of Glen Alta in 1984, St. EOM put up with the world for a little less than two more years. He continued to maintain his isolate stance and to meet his expenses by telling fortunes and filling the role of "poor man's psychiatrist." He had long ago wearied of this time-consuming sideline, as it interfered with what he considered his real vocation—making art. But in spite of this fact, he managed to continue producing powerful paintings and drawings till the end.

Boo and Nina, the two big German shepherds that had been Eddie's guard dogs and constant companions for more than 15 years, died in the late spring of 1984, and he mourned their passing as one might mourn the death of siblings, parents or a spouse. A little over a year later, in the fall of 1985, the century-old water oak that shaded the back portion of Eddie's house began showing signs of rapid decay, and after a couple of its thickest branches rotted off, he reluctantly had it cut down. In retrospect, these events seem to have foreshadowed what was to come.

Eddie's biggest problem during his last few years was his health. In that respect at least, he wasn't so different from a lot of other people his age. He had undergone double-bypass heart surgery in 1982, and he was plagued with a variety of ailments that affected his kidneys, prostate gland and inner ears. At one time he had believed his Pasaquoyan "rituals of the hair and beard" would keep him eternally young, and he was bitter about the fact that this aspect of his theory had obviously proven wrong. He was increasingly given to prolonged bouts of depression and insomnia, for which his doctors had prescribed an array of drugs like Librium, Placidyl and Nembutal.

In late 1984 he made an apparent suicide attempt, swallowing eight Nembutals in the wee hours of one of his long, sleepless nights. Scotty Steward, the young black man who worked as Eddie's cook, groundskeeper and nurse, found him unconscious early the next morning. He called an ambulance, which got Eddie to the hospital in time to revive him.

St. EOM survived two more winters after this incident. His health had consistently reached a low ebb during the winters in the years since he had turned 70. The winter of '84–'85 proved once again to be temporarily debilitating for him. But after it was over he seemed to have regained his vigor, and he made it through another seasonal cycle, including a winter, with relatively few physical complaints. Then in the spring of 1986 a recurring kidney problem landed him in the hospital in Columbus, where he underwent minor surgery and spent a compulsory week recovering.

It would be hard to find more sharply contrasting environments than Pasaquan and a modern hospital, with its depressingly sterile hallways and cubicles and people dressed in drab uniforms. Eddie had spent more than enough time in hospitals in his old age, but he apparently found this most recent experience particularly depressing. He no doubt foresaw the possibility that in the not-too-distant future he might be permanently confined to such an institution, no longer able to get about and care for himself, no longer in control of his own life. For St. EOM the thought of being uprooted from his Pasaquoyan sanctuary for good was unbearable.

Four days after he was released from the hospital, a few minutes after high noon on April 16, 1986, St. EOM took the .38-caliber pistol that he kept as last-resort protection and shot himself in the head. He had sent Scotty Steward to Buena Vista to bring back fried fish from a local restaurant for their lunch that day. But when he returned to the compound, Scotty found Eddie lying across his bed with the gun still in his hand and blood streaming from the hole in his right temple. This time he was far beyond reviving. On the table in the kitchen where Eddie had recounted the amazing story of his life for me was a one-sentence note in his unmistakable scrawl: "No one is to blame but me and my past." Draped over a nearby chair was the boldly patterned chieftan's robe from Cameroon which Eddie had recently acquired, and in which he had said he wanted to be buried when he died.

Eddie had apparently been thinking about and preparing for his death at least since 1972, when he had gone into Buena Vista one day and purchased a simple, gray coffin from the local funeral home. While he was at it, he had stopped off at the local monument company and ordered a big marble slab bearing the inscription, "ST. EOM / PA-SA-QUAN / JULY 4, 1908." The stone had lain for years on his reserved plot next to his mother's grave in the old cemetery at Ramah Primitive Baptist Church in Buena Vista.

Eddie's sister-in-law, Ruth Martin, widow of his eldest brother Julius (Jr.), made the funeral arrangements, since she was the only member of the Martin family still living in the area—only a few miles from Buena Vista in a little community called Tazewell. And Mrs. Martin wasted no time. The next day, approximately 26 hours after St. EOM performed his final act in this particular incarnation, the body was laid to rest, decked out in that regal, red-black-and-yellow African robe and beads that the

Pasaquoyan had made with his own hands out of silver and the carved stem of a mammoth *cannabis sativa* plant.

Surprisingly, about 100 people turned out at the graveside service to pay their respects, most of them family members from Florida, Alabama, Macon and Atlanta. Scattered among all these kinfolks were a few of St. EOM's fans from Buena Vista and Columbus—a couple of the area's more progressive schoolteachers, for example, and Fred Fussell, the curator at the Columbus Museum. Eddie's young assistant, Scotty Steward, was there, dressed in a black suit. I had managed, despite the short notice, to catch a flight to Columbus from North Carolina and to arrive in time to get one last look at that wise and stubborn, world-weary face, and to toss a couple of Amazon parrot feathers into the grave before it was covered over.

Ruth Martin had arranged for the pastor at her own church—a fresh-faced Baptist minister not too long out of "Bible college"—to pronounce the last rites, and it was obvious that the young preacher felt a bit out of his league eulogizing the Bodacious Mystic Badass of Buena Vista. After admitting that he had only met "Mr. Martin" on one occasion, he read a few brief passages of scripture, then, as if such a "happy ending" were required, he went on to imply that Eddie had embraced Christianity during his last days.

At that point in the brief ceremony, like a blast of admonition from the Pasaquoyan's departing spirit, a powerful gust of wind suddenly swooped down from the sky and roared through the woods at the graveyard's edge, sending a confetti-like shower of fresh dogwood-blossom petals out over the tombstones as the preacher raised his voice to be heard over the din in the treetops.

Eddie's longtime nearest neighbors David and Myrtice Nicholson, who live a half-mile from Pasaquan, were still standing by the graveside long after the funeral was over, watching the coffin as it was lowered into the ground. Myrtice, a garrulous, heavy-set woman in her seventies, explained to me as they were standing there that Eddie had once told her of an undertaker's scam he read about in the newspapers: "He said these people that ran some funeral home somewhere had been waitin' till all the mourners left the cemetery before they buried the body, then when everybody was gone they'd just open up the coffin and dump the body in the grave and take the coffin back so they could sell it again and do the same thing all over. So Eddie told me, he said, 'I don't want them to do that to me when I die. I want you to promise me that you'll come to the cemetery and stay there and watch 'em till they put the last shovelful of dirt on my grave.' "

And so Myrtice Nicholson did.

19. BLACK SON

Not long after St. EOM's funeral, I visited Pasaquan with Scotty Steward, whom I had come to know fairly well during my frequent trips there in the last years of Eddie's life. 25 years old at the time of Eddie's death, Scotty grew up in the countryside just about a mile from Pasaquan. He went to work full-time for St. EOM—or "Dude," as Scotty calls him—in 1983.

That afternoon as we walked among the temples and pagodas and totems bearing the faces of "the people of Mu," Scotty talked about the artist's last years as he had witnessed them, and about Eddie's influence on his own life:

"It was about eight years ago when I first started workin' for Dude. I was in my last year at the high school in Buena Vista, and this friend of mine named Tommy was workin' for him. Tommy was the one that got me on out here. I had seen Dude before when he'd come into town sometime, but I didn't know nothin' 'bout him. I thought he was weird, man. He looked kinda like Santa Claus. I useta be scared of him, but

Tommy said he was alright, and I needed some extra money, so I started comin' out here and rakin' leaves in the evenin' after school. And sometime he'd have me boil chinaberries in that big iron washpot over there under them pine trees. I'd build a big fire under that pot and pour them chinaberries in and boil 'em and stir 'em around, and then I'd take 'em out and peel off the skins, and he'd make beads outta the seeds.

"I worked for him on and off for the next five years. Sometime he'd have me mowin' the yard or doin' other work out on the place. I did some of the work on that last buildin' that he was workin' on that he never did finish. And then about three years ago it started gettin' where he never did want me to leave. I had another job, too, at the time. I was workin' as a cashier at the Kwickie in Buena Vista. And Dude sorta got a little bit sick one evenin', and I took him up to Doctor Sullivan and then I brought him back here. And right after we got back, I remember we was standin' out there in back by that bamboo, and he said, 'Scotty, I want you to stay with me.' He said, 'You're the only person I got. The *only* person.' I almost like to've broke down and cried, man. He had told me that I did good work and stuff like that, and that I looked like I could be trusted. But when he asked me to stay with him, I didn't know what to say. But I thought to myself, man, 'Somebody's got to take care of old people. Why shouldn't I be one of 'em?' And I told him yeah, I would stay with him. I said, 'I'll help you in any way I can.'

"He told me I had the best vibrations of any person that he had ever been around. He said some ways I reminded him of himself. He said I just looked like a honest dude. And he tried me, too. Sometime I'd be cleanin' up, and I'd find a hundred-dollar bill just layin' out on the floor. Well, I would stop what I was doin' right then, and I would go take it to him. I always felt like he put that money there just to see if I was really honest.

"Dude said I was always a person that he could rely on. He said I was his black son. I'm known around here as Scotty Martin. That's my name 'round here. When everybody sees me, I'm just like him. I be by myself. I don't fool with too many people—only the people that I know I can trust. To me, he made me what I am now. I mean, he didn't make me into a reader or nothin' like that, but he put a lotta sense up here. I'm cool about a lotta things. He taught me to be aware of everything. Sometime it scares me, man. Sometime I feel like I was too young to learn. But he was the best teacher I ever had, man.

"Sometime he'd sit at the table in there in the kitchen and tell amazin' stories, man. That would usually be in the afternoons after he'd done stopped seein' people for readin's. Most days they'd start showin' up real early in the mornin', before the sun came up. He'd get up and have his breakfast, and they'd just wait outside. Some of 'em would be here for hours, and sometime he'd decide to stop for the day. He'd tell me to tell 'em to come back later, and they'd done been out there waitin' for two or three hours. And sometime they'd tell me they'd drove a hundred or two hundred miles just to see him, but he'd tell me to tell 'em that he had to look after his own well-bein' and he was too tired to read any more that day.

"Sometime he'd tell me not to disturb him for a hour, and he'd go out there on the back porch and sit in that chair and talk to them two giant yellow faces on them columns that be lookin' at you when you walk out the back door. I'd be in the kitchen cleanin' up or readin' the paper, and he'd be out there talkin' to them two big faces. I could hear him through the window. He would be talkin' in some kinda language I couldn't understand and makin' all these wild sounds, and all these cats that live up under the house would come out and be walkin' around him and sittin' there lookin' at him and rubbin' up against his legs. And the telephone might ring, or somebody might come up out front for a readin', but I just had to tell 'em that he couldn't be disturbed right now. I never did ask him no questions about what he was doin' or what he was sayin' to them faces.

"Nobody ever bothered him the whole time I was workin' here. There was the people that come for readin's and a few that would come out just to look at the place, but nobody ever tried to break in or steal nothin' while I was here. A lotta the people around here was scared of him. I heard some people talkin' 'bout how he had these big trained rattlesnakes that lived back in the bamboo yonder, and he could call out them snakes on anybody if he wanted to. He thought it was great when I told him about that. He loved for stories like that to get around, 'cause that way people would leave him alone.

"These people in Buena Vista and around here, man, they never understood the guy, or none of his work, neither. Now that Dude's gone, they wanna get in here and look. They all wanna get in and see what's inside the house and all. They wanna know everything. That's what trips me out. 'Cause before he died, no one cared. They didn't wanna know about his health or anything like that. Now they wanna see what's here. But he really did make some place to *see,* I swear. He sure did. Inside and out.

"The last thing he had me to do that day he shot himself, before I left to go get the food for dinner, was rake up these piles of straw out there on the other side of that wall by the road. That's somethin' he used to have me to do sometime. I'd rake up all this pine straw in these four piles, and later he'd go out there and talk to these piles of straw. He'd stand there for a few minutes over each one of 'em, and he'd be talkin' and sayin' things I couldn't understand, like he was prayin' to 'em or somethin'. And he'd tell me to leave 'em there for three or four days and then spread all that straw back around on the ground again. So I thought maybe he had wanted me to do that so he could go out there and talk to them piles of straw before he shot himself.

"There was a lotta secrets he had that I knew about, but I won't ever talk about 'em, 'cause he told me never to do that. I won't never tell nobody certain things that went on here. Never in my life."

257

EPILOG

THE PAST AND THE PRESENT AND THE FUTURE COME TOGETHER

"Pasaquoyan Man in Space in the Future" is the title of a large enamel-on-wood painting which St. EOM turned out in his garret on 52nd Street in Manhattan sometime around 1950. It's an idealized self-portrait that depicts an ageless, androgynous being who hovers like the ultimate comic-book hero high in the night sky over an urban terrestrial landscape, the lights of some futuristic metropolis glowing down below. The Pasaquoyan Man is literally above it all here. His hair is of course standing straight up, antennae extended outward and tuned in to the forces of the universe, and he wears one of the pressurized, air-conditioned, levitation spacesuits which he described earlier in the text.

One afternoon more than 30 years after he executed this painting, St. EOM was asked whether he considered himself more a painter, a sculptor, an architect, a poet, a prophet or a psychic reader. To which he answered, "Well, honey, to tell you the truth, what I really am is a dam' good hustler."

It was the only time I can recall St. EOM selling himself short. The hustler's pose is an old one that Eddie Martin learned well during his youth on the New York streets—his equivalent of high school and college. But he was obviously much more than a mere hustler.

In one sense St. EOM was the archetypal reclusive mad genius. He devoted most of his life to recreating himself in his own idiosyncratic image of "the complete, natural man," and for some this may seem evidence enough of madness. But it is the evidence of his genius that screams loud and clear in eye-popping color at Pasaquan. Whatever one chooses to make of St. EOM's outrageously checkered career and his patchwork theories on ancient art and culture, it's hard not to be awestruck in the presence of this marvel built into the landscape among the Georgia pines.

Pasaquan is the culmination of Eddie Owens Martin's self-reinvention. It is his reinvention of the world—his little four-acre corner of it, anyway— and it's a remarkable achievement, one of the great masterworks of American visionary vernacular architecture. But for its creator it served as a sanctuary from a violent and corrupt modern world. The occasional sounds of the big guns going off at the nearby Fort Benning military installation are more than enough of a reminder of what St. EOM tried to isolate himself from.

"I built this place to have somethin' to identify with," said the Pasaquoyan Man, " 'cause there's nothin' I see in this society that I identify with or desire to emulate. Here I can be in my own world with my temples and designs and the spirit of God. I can have my own spirits and my own thoughts. I don't have nothin' against other people and their beliefs. I'm not askin' anybody to do my way or be my way. Although, like I said, when I'm dead and gone they'll follow like night follows day."

And so we leave St. EOM, as we found him, inside the bold-and-brazen-hued walls in the Land of Pasaquan. It's dusk on a late-summer day, and the artist is strolling among the temples and pagodas and ribbon-cane stalks, his out-of-tune guitar strapped over his shoulder. The scene resembles something out of the ancient past—a strangely garbed High Priest walking past a tall bamboo grove toward a big, bright mandala mural on a temple wall.

"In my body many spirits dwell," says the High Priest. "Past lives—people of wisdom who've experienced great things. But the main thing is, don't be afraid of life. 'Cause if you fight your true self, you'll wind up with a lotta strife."

"Men do not live once only and then depart hence forever. They live many times in many places, although not always on this world. Between each life there is a veil of darkness."

"The doors will open at last, and show us all the chambers through which our feet have wandered from the beginning."

Egyptian papyrus by Anana, Chief Scribe to King Seti II, circa 1320 B.C., as quoted in James Churchward's The Lost Continent of Mu

THE JARGON SOCIETY is a non-profit, public corporation which its founder Jonathan Williams describes as "devoted to publishing maverick poets, stray photographers, oligarchs and characters." Among its recent books have been *From This Condensery: The Complete Writing of Lorine Niedecker*; *letter in a Klein bottle* (John Menapace photographs); Paul Metcalf's *Both*; and Ernest Matthew Mickler's *White Trash Cooking*. Jargon books are distributed to bookshops by Inland Book Company, 22 Hemingway Avenue, East Haven, Connecticut 06512. Orders from individuals and libraries, requests for current catalogs and other inquiries should be directed to The Jargon Society, 1000 West Fifth Street, Winston-Salem, North Carolina 27101.